SUBLIMINAL
SPANISH

SUBLIMINAL
SPANISH

The Effortless Way to Absorb 1,000 Key Words and Phrases

LOUIS AARONS, Ph.D.

McGraw·Hill

New York   Chicago   San Francisco   Lisbon   London   Madrid   Mexico City
Milan   New Delhi   San Juan   Seoul   Singapore   Sydney   Toronto

The *McGraw·Hill* Companies

Library of Congress Cataloging-in-Publication Data

Aarons, Louis.
  Subliminal Spanish : the effortless way to absorb 1,000 key words and phrases /
Louis Aarons.
      p.   cm.
  ISBN 0-07-144351-7
    1. Spanish language—Conversation and phrase books—English.   2. Spanish
language—Glossaries, vocabularies, etc.   3. Spanish language—Self-instruction.
I. Title.

PC4121.A127   2004
468.3'421—dc22   2004055919

2 3 4 5 6 7 8 9 0   FGR/FGR   3 2 1 0 9 8 7 6 5

ISBN 0-07-144351-7 (package)
ISBN 0-07-144352-5 (book)

McGraw-Hill books are available at special quantity discounts to use as premiums and sales
promotions, or for use in corporate training programs. For more information, please write to the
Director of Special Sales, Professional Publishing, McGraw-Hill, Two Penn Plaza, New York, NY
10121-2298. Or contact your local bookstore.

This book is printed on acid-free paper.

This program is dedicated in heartfelt memory
to my beloved parents, Julia and Abraham Aarons,
who instilled in me the values of learning
and education.

Contents

CD 3

Acknowledgments

THE METHOD AND language program could not have been created without the help of many wonderful people who deserve more credit than can be expressed here.

I acknowledge with gratitude the invaluable contributions of my sons Michael, David, and John and especially my wife, Anne. Her insight on adding the visual to the auditory presentations is crucial for the method. Her verbal genius enhanced critical elements for the program. John's talent in computer programming and his brainstorming touched everything. David's perseverance was basic in text composition and his thoughts lighted nuances of the program. Michael's vocal mastery strengthened the introduction and instruction of the program and his enthusiasm sparked development.

Special thanks are owed to Joyce and Steve Aarons, Eve and Herb Retzkin, Vilma M. and Jules Aarons, Paul G. Juettner, Kathy Aarons, David Greenbaum, and Sally J. Panno-Aarons for their generous help with innumerable aspects of the programs. This program had unique help for the Spanish language by Juan De La Cruz, Alex Puga, and Karina Sanchez. The final shaping of the program could not have been accomplished without the assistance of Karen S. Young. I appreciate the support, friendship, and computer aid of my late colleague Jordan H. Lachman, M.D. I am deeply grateful to my friend David H. Witt, who was a source of encouragement, feedback, and helpful advice.

Introduction

THIS PROGRAM PROVIDES lists of words that are useful in different situations, grouped for relationships of meaning, and organized along grammatical structures. The words are then used in the context of interactive dialogues. Basic grammar is given in a brief summary at the end of the program.

The unique word arrangement speeds learning through stereo playback. Each word is heard twice: first, both the English and Spanish words; then the Spanish word. The English is on the channel for the left ear and the Spanish on the channel for the right ear. Be sure your headphones are on correctly.

Most people hear the Spanish word easier, louder, or clearer than the English word. Keep the Spanish word at the right ear. Some left-handed people may hear the Spanish better at the left ear; only they should reverse the headphones.

You may or may not hear the English words while studying. Do not try to listen to the English words; pay attention to the Spanish words.

Each list is given in a set of three different word orders. After each set of lists you will hear a tone—STOP the CD, cover the third word list, go to the self-test list, and test yourself by writing the Spanish words for the English words.

You can check your answers by looking at the third word list—the words there are in the same order as the self-test. Note any wrong answers. Go back to the start of the list, study, and retest yourself. Repeat your study until you have learned all the words.

Try to learn two or three new lists in one session or one day. Take a brief rest between new lists. At the next session, review the most recently learned lists before starting with new ones.

Dialogues are presented throughout the program to give you an idea of what the vocabulary sounds like in context. Listen to, read, and repeat aloud the dialogues to strengthen your learning of words and grammatical structures.

Grammar gives the framework of how words fit together for meaningful communication. English and Spanish have differences in their grammar. So, you'll have to be aware of the distinctions used in Spanish and ignore those you have been using in English when you want to communicate in Spanish. A summary of Spanish grammar is given near the end of the text. You should refer to the grammar section at your own pace or at least after completing your study of each CD.

These tips will help you most successfully use the program:

- *Do not try to listen to the English.* If you hear it, it's OK but *do not* try to divide your auditory attention between your ears.
- Always say the Spanish words and phrases out loud as you see and hear them—don't just read them.
- Your pronunciation will improve greatly if you also use a tape recorder often to record your own speech in Spanish. Listen to your pronunciation and compare it to that heard on the CDs.
- Feelings of progress will usually be greater at the start rather than later in the program. When you know ten words and then twenty words, you've doubled your vocabulary. After early learning, progress may seem slower.
- Many studies in learning have shown that distributed practice provides a stronger memory for the learned material compared to massed practice. For example, you may lengthen your study time by having a day of rest between lessons and find improvements in your working memory.

This program will give you a basic vocabulary and some grammar. You should supplement your studies, as needed, depending on your goal. It takes years of studying to become totally fluent in a foreign language. Fortunately, you don't have to be completely fluent to start making yourself understood in Spanish. Here are some more strategies to increase your skills:

- If you can't say exactly what you want to say, use other words. For example, if you can't say "I'd like to visit the museum," then say "I want to go to the museum."
- Use specific expressions; some of these can be taken out of the dialogues. This is an easy way to advance your conversational skills and sound more fluent. For example, **No sé, pero . . .** (*I don't know, but*) or "I don't understand, please" (you construct the Spanish). The use of such phrases will decrease pauses and allow time for you to develop your thoughts.
- Return to some of the earlier lists and dialogues and see how easy it is to repeat them now.
- Consult another introductory Spanish textbook—you'll find that you already know a lot of the material. You'll find other material that isn't in this program. This new material can now be learned easily. Indeed, if you can, get several different textbooks. Any book has its own strong and weak parts. With several books you'll get different viewpoints on the same material with a nice change in pace. When you get stuck in one, switch to another. Also, get other CDs or tapes to complement or supplement this program. Audio content is critical if you are studying alone.
- Get some children's books or comics in Spanish. Most likely you will not understand everything, but that's not a problem at this time.
- Buy a traveler's phrase book and dictionary available at most large bookstores, or check them out from your local public library. Study how words you know are combined into the different phrases.
- Listen to Spanish radio and watch Spanish TV programs.
- Visit places where Spanish is spoken, such as a Spanish grocery store. Try to hear words or phrases that are familiar to you; but don't expect to understand most of the conversations by native speakers.
- See Spanish movies without spoken English; subtitles shouldn't be a problem. Don't expect to understand very much at this point. At times the sound tracks are not very clear and they often use a lot of slang.

- Eat at a Spanish or Mexican restaurant. Check out your under-standing of the menu; if the waiter or waitress is Hispanic, try to order in Spanish. Or just say a few words and don't worry about any mistakes; they'll most likely help you and enjoy your efforts.

- Take every chance you get to use your Spanish with a native speaker of Spanish. If native speakers are not available, talk to yourself in Spanish whenever you can—bathing, walking, or driving may be good times. Recite your taped dialogues, think in Spanish about stories, or make up conversations.

- If you use a computer with an online service, communicate with members of a group or join a list that has an interest in Spanish culture or language. For example, AOL has a bulletin board on Spanish within the International House of its educa-tion section. Also, there are sites on the Internet that discuss Spanish language; e.g., http://spanish.about.com.

- Buy a bilingual dictionary and use it to enlarge your vocabu-lary. Some good dictionaries are listed in the resources section. Always write down each Spanish word that you see or read but whose meaning you do not understand. Make a list of these words on an index card. Carry the card with you and study the words while you are waiting for a train or bus or when other conditions allow this study.

You can expect some difficulties with regional accents. People will not necessarily sound like your language tapes, teacher, or radio. Further, problems often occur in using a telephone. We not only lose the higher frequencies of speech waves on the telephone but also the cues that are normally given through lip reading and body language.

Be realistic—don't expect to communicate like a native speaker of Spanish. You'll have to live in a Spanish-speaking country for some years before you will be able to come close to speaking like a native. Make up your mind how skillful you want to be and how much time you can work at it. In fact, practice is the most impor-tant way for you to make progress in learning Spanish.

Spanish Pronunciation

THE SPANISH ALPHABET has twenty-eight letters: **a, b, c, ch, d, e, f, g, h, i, j, l, ll, m, n, ñ, o, p, q, r, rr, s, t, u, v, x, y, z** (**k** and **w** only in words of foreign origin).

There are five vowels with distinct sounds:

a like <u>a</u> in *father*

e like <u>e</u> in *bet*

i like <u>i</u> in *police*

o like <u>o</u> in *vote*

u like <u>oo</u> in *fool*

The consonants, in general, do not differ greatly from their equivalents in English. However, they are not always pronounced the same in different syllable positions or letter combinations.

Some important sounds that differ from the English are:

- **b** and **v**: like an English <u>b</u> at the start of a word or after <u>m</u> or <u>n</u>; elsewhere, like English <u>v</u>, but said by bringing the lips close together
- **d**: like English at the start of a word and after <u>n</u> or <u>l</u>; elsewhere like <u>th</u> in *either*
- **h**: silent
- **ll**: like English <u>lli</u> in *million* (Northern Spain); like English <u>y</u> (Southern Spain and Americas)
- **ñ**: like English <u>ny</u> in *canyon*
- **qu**: like English <u>k</u>

- **rr**: strongly trilled, located within words
- **z**: like English <u>th</u> in *thin* (Northern Spain); like <u>s</u> in *lease* (in Southern Spain and Americas).

Spanish Accentuation

In some Spanish words, the spoken stress is marked by an accent (é): **médico, día**. However, some words with the same spelling and pronunciation use an accent mark to distinguish meaning, e.g. **si** (*if*), **sí** (*yes*).

Spanish words ending in a vowel, **-n**, or **-s** are usually stressed on the next-to-the-last syllable and on the final syllable if they end in a consonant other than **-n** or **-s**.

Now begin CD 1 and listen to the pronunciation:

a	**casa, está**
e	**mesa, este**
i	**mi, si**
o	**como, exacto**
u	**uno, segura**
v	**verano, por favor**
d	**despacio, perdone**
ll	**billete, llave**
ñ	**año, otoño**
qu	**que, querer**
h	**hijo, huevo**
rr	**correr, perro**
z	**diez, izquierdo**

Stop the CD and listen again.

Spanish Grammar

HERE ARE SOME important points to know about Spanish grammar; you can find more comprehensive information in the Grammar section at the back of the book:

Gender and Plural of Nouns

Nouns in Spanish are either masculine or feminine and are distinguished by their articles. **El** (*the*) and **un** (*a* or *an*) are used before a masculine noun. **La** (*the*) and **una** (*a* or *an*) are used before a feminine noun. For plural nouns, the masculine forms of the definite and indefinite articles, respectively, are **los** and **unos**; the feminine forms are **las** and **unas**. The indefinite plural articles, **unos** and **unas**, indicate *some*.

Nouns ending in -o are usually masculine, those ending in -a are usually feminine. Articles indicate the gender of the nouns in the printed word lists, but they are not given in the audio presentations. Write the articles on the tests to reinforce your learning of the noun gender.

Noun plurals are formed by adding -s after endings of unstressed vowels—e.g., **el hijo** (*the son*), **los hijos** (*the sons*)—and -es after consonants—e.g., **el pan** (*the bread*), **los panes** (*the breads*). Nothing is added to -es endings—e.g., **el martes** (*Tuesday*), **los martes** (*Tuesdays*).

It is important to learn the gender of the noun, because when the noun is modified by an adjective or adverb, unlike in English, the adjective or adverb changes to match the gender of the noun. For example, in English we say an *old aunt* or an *old uncle*; in Spanish, it is **una tía** (*aunt*) **vieja** or **un tío** (*uncle*) **viejo**. Also note that the Spanish adjective generally comes after the noun.

English uses the apostrophe (') to show possession; Spanish uses the preposition **de**, which means *of*; e.g., **el hijo de la mujer** (*the woman's son*—literally, *the son of the woman*).

Spanish Verbs

In English, verbs are usually designated by the word *to*, e.g., *to eat*. In Spanish, the general form of the verb is called the infinitive and ends in either **-ar**, **-er**, or **-ir**; e.g., *to speak*—**habl<u>ar</u>**; *to eat*—**com<u>er</u>**; *to live*—**viv<u>ir</u>**.

In Spanish, there are roughly three conditions for events happening in time: the present, the past, and the future. Each of these conditions is designated by changes in the endings of the verbs.

There are several verb tenses and moods in Spanish; you can find information on these in more advanced programs. Here, you will learn the main endings for verbs in the present and past and a way to speak of future events.

In English, verb forms do not change regularly with the speaker in the first and second person but do change in the third-person singular; e.g., (in the singular) *I eat, you eat, he/she eat<u>s</u>*; and (in the plural) *we eat, you eat, they eat.*

However, in Spanish the endings of the verbs change and indicate the speaker or the subject of the sentence; e.g., for *eat*: **yo** (*I*) **com<u>o</u>**, **tú** (*you*) **com<u>es</u>**, **el/ella** (*he/she*) **com<u>e</u>**, **nosotros** (*we*) **comem<u>os</u>**, **ellos/ellas** (*he/she* plural) **com<u>en</u>**. Moreover, these endings vary according to both the pattern of the infinitive verb and the tense, e.g., present, past, or future.

SUBLIMINAL
SPANISH

CD 1

Expressions and Identification
Expresiones e identificación

List 1-1

yes	sí
great	¡estupendo!
slowly	despacio
please	por favor
excuse me	perdone
that's good	está bien

List 1-2

please	por favor
that's good	está bien
slowly	despacio
yes	sí
great	¡estupendo!
excuse me	perdone

List 1-3

slowly	despacio
great	¡estupendo!
that's good	está bien
excuse me	perdone
please	por favor
yes	sí

Self-Test 1

slowly	_____
great	_____
that's good	_____
excuse me	_____
please	_____
yes	_____

Stop the CD at the tone and test yourself.

List 2-1

thank you	**gracias**
that's right	**exacto**
I'm sorry	**lo siento**
you're welcome	**de nada**
repeat that	**repita eso**
write it down	**escríbalo**

List 2-2

you're welcome	**de nada**
write it down	**escríbalo**
I'm sorry	**lo siento**
thank you	**gracias**
that's right	**exacto**
repeat that	**repita eso**

List 2-3

I'm sorry	**lo siento**
that's right	**exacto**
write it down	**escríbalo**
repeat that	**repita eso**
you're welcome	**de nada**
thank you	**gracias**

Self-Test 2

I'm sorry	_____
that's right	_____
write it down	_____
repeat that	_____
you're welcome	_____
thank you	_____

List 3-1

insurance	el **seguro**
ticket	el **billete**
last name	el **apellido**
first name	el **nombre**
address	la **dirección**
signature	la **firma**
vacation	la **vacaciones**
business	el **negocio**

List 3-2

signature	la **firma**
address	la **dirección**
business	el **negocio**
vacation	la **vacaciones**
ticket	el **billete**
insurance	el **seguro**
first name	el **nombre**
last name	el **apellido**

List 3-3

vacation	la **vacaciones**
signature	la **firma**
ticket	el **billete**
insurance	el **seguro**
first name	el **nombre**
last name	el **apellido**
address	la **dirección**
business	el **negocio**

Self-Test 3

vacation	_____
signature	_____
ticket	_____
insurance	_____
first name	_____
last name	_____
address	_____
business	_____

Time and Numbers
Tiempo y números

List 4-1

year	el **año**
month	el **mes**
spring	la **primavera**
summer	el **verano**
autumn	el **otoño**
winter	el **invierno**
today	**hoy**
what?	¿**qué**?
date	la **fecha**

List 4-2

winter	el **invierno**
autumn	el **otoño**
today	**hoy**
date	la **fecha**
what?	¿**qué**?
month	el **mes**
year	el **año**
summer	el **verano**
spring	la **primavera**

List 4-3

date	la **fecha**
winter	el **invierno**
year	el **año**
spring	la **primavera**
autumn	el **otoño**
what?	¿**qué**?
summer	el **verano**
today	**hoy**
month	el **mes**

Self-Test 4

date	_____
winter	_____
year	_____
spring	_____
autumn	_____
what?	_____
summer	_____
today	_____
month	_____

List 5-1

day	el **día**
hour	la **hora**
week	la **semana**
Monday	el **lunes**
Tuesday	el **martes**
Wednesday	el **miércoles**
Thursday	el **jueves**
Friday	el **viernes**
Saturday	el **sábado**
Sunday	el **domingo**

List 5-2

Wednesday	el **miércoles**
Tuesday	el **martes**
Monday	el **lunes**
Friday	el **viernes**
Thursday	el **jueves**
week	la **semana**
Saturday	el **sábado**
hour	la **hora**
Sunday	el **domingo**
day	el **día**

List 5-3

Saturday	el **sábado**
Thursday	el **jueves**
Sunday	el **domingo**
Wednesday	el **miércoles**
hour	la **hora**
Monday	el **lunes**
day	el **día**
week	la **semana**
Tuesday	el **martes**
Friday	el **viernes**

Self-Test 5

Saturday	_____
Thursday	_____
Sunday	_____
Wednesday	_____
hour	_____
Monday	_____
day	_____
week	_____
Tuesday	_____
Friday	_____

List 6-1

1	uno
2	dos
3	tres
4	cuatro
5	cinco
6	seis
7	siete
8	ocho
9	nueve
10	diez

List 6-2

6	seis
5	cinco
4	cuatro
8	ocho
7	siete
3	tres
9	nueve
2	dos
10	diez
1	uno

List 6-3

9	nueve
7	siete
10	diez
6	seis
2	dos
4	cuatro
1	uno
3	tres
5	cinco
8	ocho

Self-Test 6

9	_____
7	_____
10	_____
6	_____
2	_____
4	_____
1	_____
3	_____
5	_____
8	_____

List 7-1

11	once
12	doce
13	trece
14	catorce
15	quince
16	dieciséis
17	diecisiete
18	dieciocho
19	diecinueve
20	veinte

List 7-2

16	dieciséis
15	quince
14	catorce
18	dieciocho
17	diecisiete
13	trece
19	diecinueve
12	doce
20	veinte
11	once

List 7-3

19	diecinueve
17	diecisiete
20	veinte
16	dieciséis
12	doce
14	catorce
11	once
13	trece
15	quince
18	dieciocho

Self-Test 7

19	_____
17	_____
20	_____
16	_____
12	_____
14	_____
11	_____
13	_____
15	_____
18	_____

List 8-1

30	treinta
40	cuarenta
50	cincuenta
60	sesenta
70	setenta
80	ochenta
90	noventa
100	cien
1000	mil
0	cero

List 8-2

60	sesenta
50	cincuenta
40	cuarenta
80	ochenta
70	setenta
30	treinta
90	noventa
1000	mil
0	cero
100	cien

List 8-3

90	noventa
70	setenta
1000	mil
60	sesenta
100	cien
40	cuarenta
0	cero
30	treinta
50	cincuenta
80	ochenta

Self-Test 8

90	_____
70	_____
1000	_____
60	_____
100	_____
40	_____
0	_____
30	_____
50	_____
80	_____

List 9-1

January	enero
February	febrero
March	marzo
April	abril
May	mayo
June	junio
July	julio
August	agosto
September	septiembre
October	octubre
November	noviembre
December	diciembre

List 9-2

June	junio
May	mayo
April	abril
December	diciembre
September	septiembre
August	agosto
November	noviembre
March	marzo
July	julio
February	febrero
October	octubre
January	enero

List 9-3

September	septiembre
July	julio
November	noviembre
June	junio
February	febrero
April	abril
October	octubre
March	marzo
December	diciembre
January	enero
May	mayo
August	agosto

Self-Test 9

September	_____
July	_____
November	_____
June	_____
February	_____
April	_____
October	_____
March	_____
December	_____
January	_____
May	_____
August	_____

Dialogue 1A

A: What's today's date?

B: It's the ninth.

A: Yes, but what day of the week, month, and year?

B: Today is Friday, October 9, 1987.

A: That's right. Please, can you write it down? Thank you.

A: ¿Qué fecha es hoy?

B: Es el nueve.

A: Sí, ¿pero qué día de la semana, mes y año?

B: Hoy es viernes, nueve de octubre, mil novecientos ochenta y siete.

A: Exacto. Por favor, ¿puede escribirlo? Gracias.

Dialogue 1B

A: Excuse me, what time is it?

B: It's five o'clock. No, ten past five.

A: Please repeat that.

B: It's ten past five.

A: What is your name? Your first name and your last name.

B: I'm sorry. I don't understand. Can you write it down?

A: Perdone, ¿qué hora es?

B: Son las cinco. No, las cinco y diez.

A: Por favor, repita eso.

B: Son las cinco y diez.

A: ¿Cómo se llama? Su nombre y su apellido.

B: Lo siento, no comprendo. ¿Puede escribirlo?

People, Places, and Eating
Personas, lugares y comer

List 10-1

single	**soltero**
married	**casado**
wife	la **esposa**
husband	el **marido**
son	un **hijo**
cigarette	un **cigarrillo**
drink	una **bebida**
daughter	una **hija**
boyfriend	el **novio**
appointment	la **cita**

List 10-2

daughter	una **hija**
son	un **hijo**
husband	el **marido**
cigarette	un **cigarrillo**
boyfriend	el **novio**
wife	la **esposa**
appointment	la **cita**
drink	una **bebida**
married	**casado**
single	**soltero**

List 10-3

boyfriend	el **novio**
appointment	la **cita**
drink	una **bebida**
daughter	la **hija**
married	**casado**
husband	el **marido**
single	**soltero**
wife	la **esposa**
son	el **hijo**
cigarette	un **cigarrillo**

Self-Test 10

boyfriend	_____
appointment	_____
drink	_____
daughter	_____
married	_____
husband	_____
single	_____
wife	_____
son	_____
cigarette	_____

List 11-1

to speak	**hablar**
to write	**escribir**
to have	**tener**
to live	**vivir**
to be	**ser**
to be able	**poder**
north	el **norte**
south	el **sur**
east	el **este**
west	el **oeste**

List 11-2

to be able	**poder**
to be	**ser**
to live	**vivir**
south	el **sur**
north	el **norte**
to have	**tener**
east	el **este**
to write	**escribir**
west	el **oeste**
to speak	**hablar**

List 11-3

east	el **este**
north	el **norte**
west	el **oeste**
to be able	**poder**
to write	**escribir**
to live	**vivir**
to speak	**hablar**
to have	**tener**
to be	**ser**
south	el **sur**

Self-Test 11

east	_____
north	_____
west	_____
to be able	_____
to write	_____
to live	_____
to speak	_____
to have	_____
to be	_____
south	_____

List 12-1

to want	querer
to need	necesitar
to see	ver
to eat	comer
to smoke	fumar
museum	un museo
market	el mercado
toilet	el servicio
beach	la playa
post office	el correo

List 12-2

museum	un museo
to smoke	fumar
to eat	comer
toilet	el servicio
market	el mercado
to see	ver
beach	la playa
to need	necesitar
post office	el correo
to want	querer

List 12-3

beach	la playa
market	el mercado
post office	el correo
museum	un museo
to need	necesitar
to eat	comer
to want	querer
to see	ver
to smoke	fumar
toilet	el servicio

Self-Test 12

beach	_____
market	_____
post office	_____
museum	_____
to need	_____
to eat	_____
to want	_____
to see	_____
to smoke	_____
toilet	_____

List 13-1

near	cerca
far	lejos
bank	un banco
café	una cafetería
barber	un barbero
park	un parque
mailbox	un buzón
left	izquierda
right	derecha
straight on	todo recto

List 13-2

park	un parque
barber	un barbero
café	una cafetería
left	izquierda
mailbox	un buzón
bank	un banco
right	derecha
straight on	todo recto
far	lejos
near	cerca

List 13-3

right	derecha
mailbox	un buzón
straight on	todo recto
park	un parque
far	lejos
café	una cafetería
near	cerca
bank	un banco
barber	un barbero
left	izquierda

Self-Test 13

right	_____
mailbox	_____
straight on	_____
park	_____
far	_____
café	_____
near	_____
bank	_____
barber	_____
left	_____

List 14-1

there	allí
here	aquí
airport	el aeropuerto
restaurant	un restaurante
crossroads	el cruce
church	una iglesia
laundry	una lavandería
movie	un cine
hospital	un hospital
to go	ir

List 14-2

church	una iglesia
crossroads	el cruce
restaurant	un restaurante
movie	un cine
laundry	una lavandería
airport	el aeropuerto
hospital	un hospital
here	aquí
to go	ir
there	allí

List 14-3

hospital	un hospital
laundry	una lavandería
to go	ir
church	una iglesia
here	aquí
restaurant	un restaurante
there	allí
airport	el aeropuerto
crossroads	el cruce
movie	un cine

Self-Test 14

hospital	_____
laundry	_____
to go	_____
church	_____
here	_____
restaurant	_____
there	_____
airport	_____
crossroads	_____
movie	_____

Dialogue 2A

A: Excuse me, how do I get to the post office and the bank?

B: First left and then straight on.

A: Is there a barber nearby?

B: Yes, near the bank.

A: Please, can you repeat that?

B: Yes, near the bank.

A: Thank you.

A: Perdone, ¿para ir al correo y al banco?

B: La primera a la izquierda y entonces todo recto.

A: ¿Hay un barbero cerca?

B: Sí, cerca del banco.

A: Por favor, ¿puede repetir eso?

B: Sí, cerca del banco.

A: Gracias.

Dialogue 2B

A: Are you single?

B: I am married. This is my wife. Please, speak slowly.

A: Do you have any children?

B: I have a son and three daughters. This is my son. His name is Michael. My name is Louis.

A: ¿Es usted soltero?

B: Soy casado. Le presento a mi esposa. Por favor, hable despacio.

A: ¿Tiene hijos?

B: Tengo un hijo y tres hijas. Le presento a mi hijo. Se llama Miguel. Me llamo Luis.

List 15-1

bakery	la **panadería**
butcher	la **carnicería**
pharmacy	una **farmacia**
vegetable store	la **verdulería**
ice-cream parlor	la **heladería**
department store	un **almacén**
traffic light	el **semáforo**
gas station	la **gasolinera**
swimming pool	una **piscina**
dry cleaner	una **tintorería**

List 15-2

department store	un **almacén**
ice-cream parlor	la **heladería**
vegetable store	la **verdulería**
gas station	la **gasolinera**
traffic light	el **semáforo**
pharmacy	una **farmacia**
swimming pool	una **piscina**
butcher	la **carnicería**
dry cleaner	una **tintorería**
bakery	la **panadería**

List 15-3

swimming pool	una **piscina**
traffic light	el **semáforo**
dry cleaner	una **tintorería**
department store	un **almacén**
butcher	la **carnicería**
vegetable store	la **verdulería**
bakery	la **panadería**
pharmacy	una **farmacia**
ice-cream parlor	la **heladería**
gas station	la **gasolinera**

Self-Test 15

swimming pool	_____
traffic light	_____
dry cleaner	_____
department store	_____
butcher	_____
vegetable store	_____
bakery	_____
pharmacy	_____
ice-cream parlor	_____
gas station	_____

List 16-1

breakfast	el **desayuno**
lunch	la **comida**
dinner	la **cena**
coffee	un **café**
there is	**hay**
bread	el **pan**
butter	la **mantequilla**
jam	la **mermelada**
egg	un **huevo**
bill	la **cuenta**

List 16-2

bread	el **pan**
there is	**hay**
coffee	un **café**
jam	la **mermelada**
butter	la **mantequilla**
dinner	la **cena**
egg	un **huevo**
lunch	la **comida**
bill	la **cuenta**
breakfast	el **desayuno**

List 16-3

egg	un **huevo**
butter	la **mantequilla**
bill	la **cuenta**
bread	el **pan**
lunch	la **comida**
coffee	un **café**
breakfast	el **desayuno**
dinner	la **cena**
there is	**hay**
jam	la **mermelada**

Self-Test 16

egg	_____
butter	_____
bill	_____
bread	_____
lunch	_____
coffee	_____
breakfast	_____
dinner	_____
there is	_____
jam	_____

Dialogue 3A

A: Excuse me, how do I get to a café?

B: Straight ahead.

A: I want to eat breakfast—bread and eggs. Is there a park nearby?

B: Yes, to the right.

A: Is there a department store there?

B: No, I'm sorry.

A: That's okay. I want to see the park.

A: **Perdone, ¿para ir a la cafetería?**

B: **Todo recto.**

A: **Quiero comer desayuno—pan y huevos. ¿Hay un parque cerca?**

B: **Sí, a la derecha.**

A: **¿Hay un almacén allí?**

B: **No, lo siento.**

A: **Está bien. Quiero ver el parque.**

Dialogue 3B

A: Please, have you got a list of restaurants?

B: I'm sorry, no.

A: May one smoke here?

B: I'm sorry, no.

A: That's okay, is there a toilet nearby?

B: Yes, there to the right.

A: Thank you.

B: You're welcome.

A: **Por favor, ¿tiene una lista de restaurantes?**

B: **Lo siento, no.**

A: **¿Se puede fumar aquí?**

B: **Lo siento, no.**

A: **Está bien, ¿hay un servicio cerca?**

B: **Sí, allá a la derecha.**

A: **Gracias.**

B: **De nada.**

Lodging
Alojamiento

List 17-1

house	la **casa**
room	la **habitación**
bed	la **cama**
shower	la **ducha**
cot	un **catre**
bathroom	el **baño**
night	una **noche**
key	la **llave**
blanket	una **manta**
pillow	la **almohada**

List 17-2

bathroom	el **baño**
cot	un **catre**
shower	la **ducha**
key	la **llave**
night	una **noche**
bed	la **cama**
room	la **habitación**
pillow	la **almohada**
house	la **casa**
blanket	una **manta**

List 17-3

room	la **habitación**
night	una **noche**
bathroom	el **baño**
blanket	una **manta**
bed	la **cama**
pillow	la **almohada**
house	la **casa**
shower	la **ducha**
cot	un **catre**
key	la **llave**

Self-Test 17

room	_____
night	_____
bathroom	_____
blanket	_____
bed	_____
pillow	_____
house	_____
shower	_____
cot	_____
key	_____

List 18-1

quiet	tranquila
glass	un vaso
soap	el jabón
come in	¡adelante!
towel	una toalla
ashtray	un cenicero
receipt	el recibo
deposit	la finanza
water	el agua
luggage	el equipaje

List 18-2

towel	una toalla
come in	¡adelante!
luggage	el equipaje
ashtray	un cenicero
receipt	el recibo
soap	el jabón
deposit	la finanza
water	el agua
quiet	tranquila
glass	el vaso

List 18-3

deposit	la finanza
receipt	el recibo
luggage	el equipaje
towel	una toalla
glass	un vaso
come in	¡adelante!
quiet	tranquila
soap	el jabón
ashtray	un cenicero
water	el agua

Self-Test 18

deposit	_____
receipt	_____
luggage	_____
towel	_____
glass	_____
come in	_____
quiet	_____
soap	_____
ashtray	_____
water	_____

List 19-1

telephone	el **teléfono**
store	la **tienda**
kitchen	la **cocina**
electricity	la **electricidad**
iron	la **plancha**
broom	una **escoba**
refrigerator	la **nevera**
can opener	un **abrelatas**
light bulb	la **bombilla**
washer	la **lavadora**

List 19-2

broom	una **escoba**
iron	la **plancha**
electricity	la **electricidad**
can opener	un **abrelatas**
refrigerator	la **nevera**
kitchen	la **cocina**
light bulb	la **bombilla**
store	la **tienda**
washer	la **lavadora**
telephone	el **teléfono**

List 19-3

light bulb	la **bombilla**
refrigerator	la **nevera**
washer	la **lavadora**
broom	una **escoba**
store	la **tienda**
electricity	la **electricidad**
telephone	el **teléfono**
kitchen	la **cocina**
iron	la **plancha**
can opener	un **abrelatas**

Self-Test 19

light bulb	_____
refrigerator	_____
washer	_____
broom	_____
store	_____
electricity	_____
telephone	_____
kitchen	_____
iron	_____
can opener	_____

List 20-1

knife	un **cuchillo**
fork	un **tenedor**
spoon	una **cuchara**
plate	un **plato**
napkin	una **servilleta**
frying pan	una **sartén**
sink	el **fregadero**
rubbish	la **basura**
to be	**estar**
town	la **ciudad**

List 20-2

frying pan	una **sartén**
napkin	una **servilleta**
plate	un **plato**
to be	**estar**
rubbish	la **basura**
spoon	una **cuchara**
fork	un **tenedor**
sink	el **fregadero**
town	la **ciudad**
knife	un **cuchillo**

List 20-3

to be	**estar**
sink	el **fregadero**
town	la **ciudad**
frying pan	una **sartén**
fork	un **tenedor**
plate	un **plato**
knife	un **cuchillo**
spoon	una **cuchara**
napkin	una **servilleta**
rubbish	la **basura**

Self-Test 20

to be	_____
sink	_____
town	_____
frying pan	_____
fork	_____
plate	_____
knife	_____
spoon	_____
napkin	_____
rubbish	_____

Dialogue 4A

A: I would like a quiet room
with two beds and a bath-
room.

B: Please, come in!

A: It's for three nights. Is
there a restaurant?

B: Yes.

A: What time is dinner?

B: From seven o'clock
onwards.

A: Great! I want to see the
room.

A: Quiero una habitación
tranquila con dos camas
y baño.

B: Por favor, ¡adelante!

A: Es para tres noches. ¿Hay
restaurante?

B: Sí.

A: ¿A qué hora es la cena?

B: Desde las siete en
adelante.

A: ¡Estupendo! Quiero ver
la habitación.

Dialogue 4B

A: I am in town, may I
reserve a room?

B: How many nights is it for?

A: It's for one week. I would
like a double bed and a
shower.

B: Do you want to see the
room?

A: No, thank you, but does it
have a kitchen with a
refrigerator?

A: Estoy en la ciudad,
¿puedo reservar una
habitación?

B: ¿Para cuántas noches es?

A: Es para una semana.
Quiero una cama doble y
una ducha.

B: ¿Quiere ver la
habitación?

A: No, gracias, ¿pero tiene
una cocina con nevera?

Pharmacy
Farmacia

List 21-1

aspirin	las **aspirinas**
bandage	una **venda**
sting	una **picadura**
burn	una **quemadura**
cold	el **catarro**
constipation	el **estreñimiento**
cough	la **tos**
sprain	la **torcedura**
flu	la **gripe**
diarrhea	la **diarrea**

List 21-2

constipation	el **estreñimiento**
burn	una **quemadura**
cold	el **catarro**
sprain	la **torcedura**
cough	la **tos**
sting	una **picadura**
flu	la **gripe**
bandage	una **venda**
diarrhea	la **diarrea**
aspirin	las **aspirinas**

List 21-3

flu	la **gripe**
cough	la **tos**
diarrhea	la **diarrea**
constipation	el **estreñimiento**
bandage	una **venda**
burn	una **quemadura**
aspirin	las **aspirinas**
sting	una **picadura**
cold	el **catarro**
sprain	la **torcedura**

Self-Test 21

flu	_____
cough	_____
diarrhea	_____
constipation	_____
bandage	_____
burn	_____
aspirin	_____
sting	_____
cold	_____
sprain	_____

List 22-1

toilet paper	el **papel higiénico**
razor blades	unas **cuchillas**
toothpaste	la **pasta de dientes**
deodorant	un **desodorante**
soft	**suave**
to buy	**comprar**
to get	**obtener**
where?	¿**dónde**?
how much?	¿**cuánto**?
something	**algo**

List 22-2

to buy	**comprar**
soft	**suave**
deodorant	un **desodorante**
where?	¿**dónde**?
to get	**obtener**
toothpaste	la **pasta de dientes**
how much?	¿**cuánto**?
razor blades	unas **cuchillas**
something	**algo**
toilet paper	el **papel higiénico**

List 22-3

how much?	¿**cuánto**?
to get	**obtener**
something	**algo**
to buy	**comprar**
razor blades	unas **cuchillas**
deodorant	un **desodorante**
toilet paper	el **papel higiénico**
toothpaste	la **pasta de dientes**
soft	**suave**
where?	¿**dónde**?

Self-Test 22

how much	_____
to get	_____
something	_____
to buy	_____
razor blades	_____
deodorant	_____
toilet paper	_____
toothpaste	_____
soft	_____
where?	_____

List 23-1

newspaper	un **periódico**
envelopes	los **sobres**
guidebook	una **guía**
map	un **plano**
umbrella	un **paraguas**
camera	una **cámara**
postcards	las **postales**
sunglasses	las **gafas de sol**
matches	las **cerillas**
suitcase	la **maleta**

List 23-2

camera	una **cámara**
umbrella	un **paraguas**
map	un **plano**
sunglasses	las **gafas de sol**
postcards	las **postales**
guidebook	una **guía**
matches	las **cerillas**
envelopes	los **sobres**
suitcase	la **maleta**
newspaper	un **periódico**

List 23-3

matches	las **cerillas**
postcards	las **postales**
suitcase	la **maleta**
camera	una **cámara**
envelopes	los **sobres**
map	un **plano**
newspaper	un **periódico**
guidebook	una **guía**
umbrella	un **paraguas**
sunglasses	las **gafas de sol**

Self-Test 23

matches	_____
postcards	_____
suitcase	_____
camera	_____
envelopes	_____
map	_____
newspaper	_____
guidebook	_____
umbrella	_____
sunglasses	_____

Dialogue 5A

A: Where can I get something for a cold? Where is the drugstore?

B: It's far, it's in the town.

A: Thank you, that's good. I need razor blades and soft paper tissues. Also, I want something for a cough.

A: ¿Dónde puedo obtener algo para el catarro? ¿Dónde está la farmacia?

B: Está lejos, está en la ciudad.

A: Gracias, está bien. Necesito cuchillas y suave tisús. También, quiero algo para la tos.

Dialogue 5B

A: Where can I buy a camera?

B: In the pharmacy at the department store.

A: Thank you. I also need cigarettes, matches, and a newspaper, and a map of the town.

B: You can buy everything at the pharmacy.

A: ¿Dónde puedo comprar una cámara?

B: En la farmacia del almacén.

A: Gracias. También necesito cigarrillos, cerillas y un periódico, y plano de la ciudad.

B: Puede comprar todo en la farmacia.

Clothing
Ropa

List 24-1

hat	el **sombrero**
coat	el **abrigo**
cap	el **gorro**
belt	un **cinturón**
pants	los **pantalones**
shirt	la **camisa**
jeans	los **vaqueros**
socks	los **calcetines**
suit	el **traje**
T-shirt	una **camiseta**

List 24-2

shirt	la **camisa**
pants	los **pantalones**
belt	un **cinturón**
jeans	los **vaqueros**
T-shirt	una **camiseta**
cap	el **gorro**
socks	los **calcetines**
coat	el **abrigo**
hat	el **sombrero**
suit	el **traje**

List 24-3

socks	los **calcetines**
T-shirt	una **camiseta**
suit	el **traje**
shirt	la **camisa**
coat	el **abrigo**
belt	un **cinturón**
hat	el **sombrero**
cap	el **gorro**
pants	los **pantalones**
jeans	los **vaqueros**

Self-Test 24

socks	_____
T-shirt	_____
suit	_____
shirt	_____
coat	_____
belt	_____
hat	_____
cap	_____
pants	_____
jeans	_____

List 25-1

bathrobe	la **bata**
blouse	una **blusa**
bra	un **sujetador**
panties	unas **bragas**
stockings	las **medias**
nightgown	un **camisón**
skirt	una **falda**
dress	un **vestido**
jacket	una **chaqueta**
raincoat	un **impermeable**

List 25-2

nightgown	un **camisón**
stockings	las **medias**
panties	unas **bragas**
dress	un **vestido**
skirt	una **falda**
bra	un **sujetador**
jacket	una **chaqueta**
blouse	una **blusa**
raincoat	un **impermeable**
bathrobe	la **bata**

List 25-3

jacket	una **chaqueta**
skirt	una **falda**
raincoat	un **impermeable**
nightgown	un **camisón**
stockings	las **medias**
blouse	una **blusa**
panties	unas **bragas**
bathrobe	la **bata**
bra	un **sujetador**
dress	un **vestido**

Self-Test 25

jacket	_____
skirt	_____
raincoat	_____
nightgown	_____
stockings	_____
blouse	_____
panties	_____
bathrobe	_____
bra	_____
dress	_____

List 26-1

underdrawers	los **calzoncillos**
measurements	las **medidas**
shoes	los **zapatos**
sandals	las **sandalias**
boots	las **botas**
moccasins	los **mocasines**
size (garment)	la **talla**
gift	un **regalo**
pair	un **par**
gloves	unos **guantes**

List 26-2

moccasins	los **mocasines**
boots	las **botas**
sandals	las **sandalias**
gift	un **regalo**
size (garment)	la **talla**
shoes	los **zapatos**
pair	un **par**
measurements	las **medidas**
gloves	unos **guantes**
underdrawers	los **calzoncillos**

List 26-3

pair	un **par**
size (garment)	la **talla**
gloves	unos **guantes**
moccasins	los **mocasines**
measurements	las **medidas**
sandals	las **sandalias**
underdrawers	los **calzoncillos**
shoes	los **zapatos**
boots	las **botas**
gift	un **regalo**

Self-Test 26

pair	_____
size (garment)	_____
gloves	_____
moccasins	_____
measurements	_____
sandals	_____
underdrawers	_____
shoes	_____
boots	_____
gift	_____

Dialogue 6A

A: Where is a department
   store? I want to buy an
   umbrella, sunglasses, and
   a hat.

B: It's near the market.

A: Great! I need gloves, size
   eight, for a gift. Also, a
   pair of shoes.

Dialogue 6B

A: I'd like a raincoat, my size
   is forty.

B: I don't have it, I'm sorry.

A: I'd like a pair of shoes,
   my size is eight, and two
   pairs of socks. How much
   is it?

B: $70.

A: That's good.

A: ¿Dónde están unos
   almacenes? Quiero
   comprar un paraguas,
   unas gafas de sol, y un
   sombrero.

B: Está cerca del mercado.

A: ¡Estupendo! Necesito
   guantes, talla ocho, para
   un regalo. También, un
   par de zapatos.

A: Quiero un impermeable,
   mi talla es cuarenta.

B: No tengo, lo siento.

A: Quiero un par de
   zapatos, mi número es
   ocho, y dos pares de
   calcetines. ¿Cuánto es?

B: Sesenta dólares.

A: Está bien.

List 27-1

collar	el **cuello**
hip	la **cadera**
leg	la **pierna**
waist	la **cintura**
wool	la **lana**
suede	el **ante**
nylon	el **nilón**
leather	el **cuero**
denim	el **dril**
cotton	el **algodón**

List 27-2

suede	el **ante**
wool	la **lana**
waist	la **cintura**
leather	el **cuero**
nylon	el **nilón**
leg	la **pierna**
denim	el **dril**
hip	la **cadera**
cotton	el **algodón**
collar	el **cuello**

List 27-3

denim	el **dril**
nylon	el **nilón**
cotton	el **algodón**
suede	el **ante**
wool	la **lana**
hip	la **cadera**
waist	la **cintura**
collar	el **cuello**
leg	la **pierna**
leather	el **cuero**

Self-Test 27

denim	_____
nylon	_____
cotton	_____
suede	_____
wool	_____
hip	_____
waist	_____
collar	_____
leg	_____
leather	_____

List 28-1

black	**negro**
white	**blanco**
gray	**gris**
red	**rojo**
yellow	**amarillo**
blue	**azul**
green	**verde**
pink	**rosa**
brown	**moreno**
orange	**naranja**

List 28-2

blue	**azul**
yellow	**amarillo**
red	**rojo**
pink	**rosa**
green	**verde**
gray	**gris**
brown	**moreno**
white	**blanco**
orange	**naranja**
black	**negro**

List 28-3

brown	**moreno**
green	**verde**
orange	**naranja**
blue	**azul**
white	**blanco**
red	**rojo**
black	**negro**
gray	**gris**
yellow	**amarillo**
pink	**rosa**

Self-Test 28

brown	_____
green	_____
orange	_____
blue	_____
white	_____
red	_____
black	_____
gray	_____
yellow	_____
pink	_____

List 29-1

enough	**basta**
more	**más**
less	**menos**
better	**mejor**
cheaper	**más barato**
different	**diferente**
larger	**más grande**
smaller	**más pequeño**
open	**abierto**
closed	**cerrado**

List 29-2

different	**diferente**
cheaper	**más barato**
better	**mejor**
smaller	**más pequeño**
larger	**más grande**
less	**menos**
open	**abierto**
more	**más**
closed	**cerrado**
enough	**basta**

List 29-3

open	**abierto**
larger	**más grande**
closed	**cerrado**
different	**diferente**
more	**más**
better	**mejor**
enough	**basta**
less	**menos**
cheaper	**más barato**
smaller	**más pequeño**

Self-Test 29

open	_____
larger	_____
closed	_____
different	_____
more	_____
better	_____
enough	_____
less	_____
cheaper	_____
smaller	_____

Dialogue 7A

A: I need a dress. Have you got something in yellow cotton?

B: Yes, I have.

A: These are the measurements, collar twelve, bust thirty-four, waist twenty-six, and hip thirty-five. Have you got something cheaper?

A: Necesito un vestido. ¿Tiene algo de algodón en amarillo?

B: Sí, tengo.

A: Éstas son las medidas, cuello doce, busto treinta y cuatro, cintura vientiséis, y cadera treinta y cinco. ¿Tiene algo más barato?

Dialogue 7B

A: I'd like a suit. Have you got something in blue wool?

B: Yes, I have.

A: How much is this?

B: $200.

A: Have you got something different and better?

B: Yes, a suit of gray suede.

A: When do you close?

B: At five forty-five.

A: Quiero un traje. ¿Tiene algo de lana en azul?

B: Sí, tengo.

A: ¿Cuánto cuesta esto?

B: Doscientos dólares.

A: ¿Tiene algo diferente y mejor?

B: Sí, un traje de ante en gris.

A: ¿A qué hora cierran?

B: A las seis menos cuarto.

Food
Comida

List 30-1

pastries	las **pastas**
cake	la **torta**
slice ~~*piece*~~	un **trozo**
ice cream	un **helado**
cone	un **barquillo**
chocolate	el **chocolate**
vanilla	la **vainilla**
strawberry	la **fresa**
pistachio	el **mantecado**
when?	¿**cuándo**?

List 30-2

chocolate	el **chocolate**
cone	un **barquillo**
ice cream	un **helado**
strawberry	la **fresa**
vanilla	la **vainilla**
slice	un **trozo**
pistachio	el **mantecado**
cake	la **torta**
when?	¿**cuándo**?
pastries	las **pastas**

List 30-3

pistachio	el **mantecado**
vanilla	la **vainilla**
when?	¿**cuándo**?
chocolate	el **chocolate**
cake	la **torta**
ice cream	un **helado**
pastries	las **pastas**
slice ~~*piece*~~	un **trozo**
cone	un **barquillo**
strawberry	la **fresa**

Self-Test 30

pistachio	_____
vanilla	_____
when?	_____
chocolate	_____
cake	_____
ice cream	_____
pastries	_____
slice	_____
cone	_____
strawberry	_____

List 31-1

frozen foods	los **congelados**
chewing gum	un **chicle**
cheese	el **queso**
fish	el **pescado**
to serve	**servir**
meat	la **carne**
milk	la **leche**
salt	la **sal**
sugar	el **azúcar**
self-service	el **autoservicio**

List 31-2

meat	la **carne**
to serve	**servir**
fish	el **pescado**
salt	la **sal**
milk	la **leche**
cheese	el **queso**
sugar	el **azúcar**
chewing gum	un **chicle**
self-service	el **autoservicio**
frozen foods	los **congelados**

List 31-3

sugar	el **azúcar**
milk	la **leche**
self-service	el **autoservicio**
meat	la **carne**
chewing gum	un **chicle**
fish	el **pescado**
frozen foods	los **congelados**
cheese	el **queso**
to serve	**servir**
salt	la **sal**

Self-Test 31

sugar	_____
milk	_____
self-service	_____
meat	_____
chewing gum	_____
fish	_____
frozen foods	_____
cheese	_____
to serve	_____
salt	_____

List 32-1

delicatessen	la mantequería
entrance	la entrada
exit	la salida
check-out	la caja
cold cuts	los fiambres
seafood	los mariscos
salami	el salchichón
tuna	el atún
ham	el jamón
biscuits	las galletas

List 32-2

seafood	los mariscos
cold cuts	los fiambres
check-out	la caja
tuna	el atún
salami	el salchichón
exit	la salida
ham	el jamón
entrance	la entrada
biscuits	las galletas
delicatessen	la mantequería

List 32-3

ham	el jamón
salami	el salchichón
biscuits	las galletas
seafood	los mariscos
entrance	la entrada
check-out	la caja
delicatessen	la mantequería
exit	la salida
cold cuts	los fiambres
tuna	el atún

Self-Test 32

ham	_____
salami	_____
cookies	_____
seafood	_____
entrance	_____
check-out	_____
delicatessen	_____
exit	_____
cold cuts	_____
tuna	_____

List 33-1

vegetables	las **legumbres**
carrots	las **zanahorias**
peas	unos **guisantes**
corn	el **maíz**
beans (kidney)	las **judías**
potatoes	unas **patatas**
tomatoes	unos **tomates**
lettuce	una **lechuga**
spinach	la **espinaca**
asparagus	el **espárrago**

List 33-2

potatoes	unas **patatas**
beans (kidney)	las **judías**
corn	el **maíz**
lettuce	una **lechuga**
tomatoes	unos **tomates**
peas	unos **guisantes**
spinach	la **espinaca**
carrots	las **zanahorias**
asparagus	el **espárrago**
vegetables	las **legumbres**

List 33-3

spinach	la **espinaca**
tomatoes	unos **tomates**
asparagus	el **espárrago**
potatoes	unas **patatas**
carrots	las **zanahorias**
corn	el **maíz**
vegetables	las **legumbres**
peas	unos **guisantes**
lettuce	una **lechuga**
beans (kidney)	las **judías**

Self-Test 33

spinach	_____
tomatoes	_____
asparagus	_____
potatoes	_____
carrots	_____
corn	_____
vegetables	_____
peas	_____
lettuce	_____
beans (kidney)	_____

Review Test 1

You heard, read, repeated, and wrote the words in this program for maximum learning. People differ in ability and study schedules and their memory differs for specific words. Words not used may be forgotten, but are relearned quickly. Your learning will be stronger if you review your memory of words from all the lists and restudy those you have forgotten.

Two words from each list are given below. Write the Spanish word for the English word and check your answers. Relearn each list wherever both words are missed from the same list. If only one word is missed, look at the list and see if you need to restudy it.

Your memory of the words will be maintained and fluency will increase by using them when you speak Spanish.

List	Test Words	Answer
1	slowly	_despacio_
	excuse me	_disculpe_
2	I'm sorry	_lo siento_
	write it down	_escribelo_
3	signature	_firma_
	business	_negocio_
4	summer	_verano_
	winter	_invierno_
5	Friday	_viernes_
	Tuesday	_martes_
6	5	_cinco_
	7	_siete_
7	11	_once_
	20	_veinte_

List	Test Words	Answer *(continued)*
8	50	*cincuenta*
	100	*cien*
9	January	*enero*
	March	*mayo*
10	drink	*dish*
	husband	
11	south	*sur*
	east	
12	to see	
	market	
13	park	*pharmacy*
	far	*typ*
14	movie	*cine*
	laundry	
15	bakery	
	butcher	
16	jam	
	butter	
17	blanket	
	pillow	
18	towel	
	soap	
19	broom	
	kitchen	
20	spoon	
	knife	

List	Test Words	Answer (continued)
21	constipation	_____
	flu	_____
22	deodorant	_____
	to buy	_____
23	guidebook	_____
	postcards	_____
24	coat	_____
	belt	_____
25	skirt	_____
	blouse	_____
26	boots	_____
	pair	_____
27	leather	_____
	denim	_____
28	red	_____
	brown	_____
29	enough	_____
	open	_____
30	when?	_____
	cake	_____
31	fish	_____
	salt	_____
32	cold cuts	_____
	seafood	_____
33	lettuce	_____
	spinach	_____

CD 2

List 34-1

fruit	la **fruta**
apples	unas **manzanas**
oranges	unas **naranjas**
pears	unas **peras**
bananas	unos **plátanos**
peaches	los **melocotones**
grapes	unas **uvas**
cherries	unas **cerezas**
plums	unas **ciruelas**
grapefruit	un **pomelo**

List 34-2

peaches	los **melocotones**
bananas	unos **plátanos**
pears	unas **peras**
cherries	unas **cerezas**
grapes	unas **uvas**
oranges	unas **naranjas**
plums	unas **ciruelas**
apples	unas **manzanas**
grapefruit	un **pomelo**
fruit	la **fruta**

List 34-3

plums	unas **ciruelas**
grapes	unas **uvas**
grapefruit	un **pomelo**
peaches	los **melocotones**
apples	unas **manzanas**
pears	unas **peras**
fruit	la **fruta**
oranges	unas **naranjas**
bananas	unos **plátanos**
cherries	unas **cerezas**

Self-Test 34

plums	_____
grapes	_____
grapefruit	_____
peaches	_____
apples	_____
pears	_____
fruit	_____
oranges	_____
bananas	_____
cherries	_____

Dialogue 8A

A: Can I help you?

B: I'd like to eat fruit and vegetables. I need to buy apples, grapes, bananas, carrots, peas, and potatoes. Excuse me, where is the check-out and the exit?

A: There, to the right.

B: Thank you.

A: ¿En qué puedo servirle?

B: Quiero comer frutas y legumbres. Necesito comprar manzanas, uvas, platános, zanahorias, guisantes y papas. Perdone, ¿dónde está la caja y la salida?

B: Allí, a la derecha.

A: Gracias.

Dialogue 8B

A: I'd like some pastries and ice cream. Please, a piece of chocolate cake and a strawberry cone.

B: Anything else?

A: No, thank you. When do you close?

B: In half an hour.

A: Quiero unas pastas y un helado. Por favor, un trozo de torta de chocolate y un barquillo de fresa.

B: ¿Algo más?

A: No, gracias. ¿A qué hora cierran?

B: En media hora.

List 35-1

beef	el **buey**
lamb	el **cordero**
pork	el **cerdo**
veal	la **ternera**
steak	un **bistec**
liver	el **hígado**
sausage	una **salchicha**
chops	unas **chuletas**
chicken	un **pollo**
rabbit	un **conejo**

List 35-2

liver	el **hígado**
steak	un **bistec**
veal	la **ternera**
chops	unas **chuletas**
sausage	una **salchicha**
pork	el **cerdo**
chicken	un **pollo**
lamb	el **cordero**
rabbit	un **conejo**
beef	el **buey**

List 35-3

chicken	un **pollo**
sausage	una **salchicha**
rabbit	un **conejo**
liver	el **hígado**
lamb	el **cordero**
veal	la **ternera**
beef	el **buey**
pork	el **cerdo**
steak	un **bistec**
chops	unas **chuletas**

Self-Test 35

chicken	_____
sausage	_____
rabbit	_____
liver	_____
lamb	_____
veal	_____
beef	_____
pork	_____
steak	_____
chops	_____

List 36-1

sole	el **lenguado**
herring	un **arenque**
trout	una **trucha**
lobster	una **langosta**
crab	un **cangrejo**
clams	unas **almejas**
cod	el **bacalao**
shrimp	unos **camarones**
salmon	el **salmón**
turbot	un **rodaballo**

List 36-2

clams	unas **almejas**
crab	un **cangrejo**
lobster	una **langosta**
shrimp	unos **camarones**
cod	el **bacalao**
trout	una **trucha**
salmon	el **salmón**
herring	un **arenque**
turbot	un **rodaballo**
sole	el **lenguado**

List 36-3

salmon	el **salmón**
cod	un **bacalao**
turbot	el **rodaballo**
clams	unas **almejas**
herring	un **arenque**
lobster	una **langosta**
sole	el **lenguado**
trout	una **trucha**
crab	un **cangrejo**
shrimp	unos **camarones**

Self-Test 36

salmon	_____
cod	_____
turbot	_____
clams	_____
herring	_____
lobster	_____
sole	_____
trout	_____
crab	_____
shrimp	_____

Dialogue 9A

A: I would like to buy some sausages, three lamb chops, and chicken. Then I'd like to eat. Where is a butcher shop and a café?

B: The butcher shop is in the town, near the delicatessen.

A: Thank you.

A: Quiero comprar salchichas, tres chuletas de cordero y pollo. Entonces, quiero comer. ¿Dondé está una carnicería y una cafetería?

B: La carnicería está en la ciudad, cerca de la mantequería.

A: Gracias.

Dialogue 9B

A: I would like to buy five slices of salmon and cod, also a herring. Where is a fish store?

B: There is a fish store in the market, near the traffic light.

A: Thank you.

B: You're welcome

A: Quiero comprar cinco rodajas de salmón y bacalao, también un arenque. ¿Dondé está una pescadería?

B: Hay una pescadería en el mercado, cerca del semáforo.

A: Gracias.

B: De nada.

Refreshments
Refrescos

List 37-1

milk shake	un **batido**
cider	una **sidra**
lemonade	una **limonada**
black coffee	un **café solo**
waiter	el **camarero**
beer	una **cerveza**
gin	una **ginebra**
brandy	un **coñac**
whiskey	un **whisky**
rum	un **ron**

List 37-2

beer	una **cerveza**
waiter	el **camarero**
black coffee	un **café solo**
brandy	un **coñac**
gin	una **ginebra**
lemonade	una **limonada**
whiskey	un **whisky**
cider	una **sidra**
rum	un **ron**
milk shake	un **batido**

List 37-3

whiskey	un **whisky**
gin	una **ginebra**
rum	un **ron**
beer	una **cerveza**
cider	una **sidra**
black coffee	un **café solo**
milk shake	un **batido**
lemonade	una **limonada**
waiter	el **camarero**
brandy	un **coñac**

Self-Test 37

whiskey	_____
gin	_____
rum	_____
beer	_____
cider	_____
black coffee	_____
milk shake	_____
lemonade	_____
waiter	_____
brandy	_____

List 38-1

dry	seco
sweet	dulce
bottle	una botella
with ice	con hielo
sandwich	un bocadillo
soup	la sopa
hot	caliente
bacon	el tocino
appetizers	las tapas
custard	las natillas

List 38-2

soup	la sopa
sandwich	un bocadillo
with ice	con hielo
bacon	el tocino
hot	caliente
bottle	una botella
appetizers	las tapas
sweet	dulce
custard	las natillas
dry	seco

List 38-3

appetizers	las tapas
hot	caliente
custard	las natillas
soup	la sopa
sweet	dulce
with ice	con hielo
dry	seco
bottle	una botella
sandwich	un bocadillo
bacon	el tocino

Self-Test 38

appetizers	_____
hot	_____
custard	_____
soup	_____
sweet	_____
with ice	_____
dry	_____
bottle	_____
sandwich	_____
bacon	_____

Dialogue 10A

A: Waiter, I'd like a glass of lemonade with ice please.

B: Would you also like a sandwich?

A: Yes, a salami sandwich and some hot soup. The bill please. How much is it?

B: Five dollars.

A: Thank you.

B: You're welcome.

A: Camarero, quiero un vaso de limonada con hielo, por favor.

B: ¿Quiere un bocadillo también?

A: Sí, un bocadillo de salchichón y sopa caliente. La cuenta por favor. ¿Cuánto es?

B: Cinco dólares.

A: Gracias.

B: De nada.

Dialogue 10B

A: Waitress, do you have appetizers?

B: Yes, anything else?

A: We'd like two beers and two ham sandwiches. How much is it?

B: Four dollars.

A: Is service included?

A: Yes.

A: Camarera, ¿tiene las tapas?

B: Sí, ¿algo más?

A: Queremos dos cervezas y dos bocadillos de jamón. ¿Cuánto es?

B: Cuatro dólares.

A: ¿Está el servicio incluido?

B: Sí.

The Human Body and Illness
El cuerpo humano y la enfermedad

List 39-1

ear	el **oído**
eye	el **ojo**
head	la **cabeza**
jaw	la **mandíbula**
neck	el **cuello**
throat	la **garganta**
arm	el **brazo**
back	la **espalda**
shoulder	el **hombro**
wrist	la **muñeca**

List 39-2

throat	la **garganta**
neck	el **cuello**
jaw	la **mandíbula**
back	la **espalda**
arm	el **brazo**
head	la **cabeza**
shoulder	el **hombro**
eye	el **ojo**
wrist	la **muñeca**
ear	el **oído**

List 39-3

shoulder	el **hombro**
arm	el **brazo**
wrist	la **muñeca**
throat	la **garganta**
eye	el **ojo**
jaw	la **mandíbula**
ear	el **oído**
head	la **cabeza**
neck	el **cuello**
back	la **espalda**

Self-Test 39

shoulder	_____
arm	_____
wrist	_____
throat	_____
eye	_____
jaw	_____
ear	_____
head	_____
neck	_____
back	_____

List 40-1

foot	el **pie**
heel	el **talón**
stomach	el **estómago**
lung	el **pulmón**
dentures	la **dentadura**
filling	un **empaste**
dentist	un **dentista**
ill	**enfermo**
dizzy	**mareado**
weak	**débil**

List 40-2

filling	un **empaste**
dentures	la **dentadura**
lung	el **pulmón**
ill	**enfermo**
dentist	un **dentista**
stomach	el **estómago**
dizzy	**mareado**
heel	el **talón**
weak	**débil**
foot	el **pie**

List 40-3

dizzy	**mareado**
dentist	un **dentista**
weak	**débil**
filling	un **empaste**
heel	el **talón**
lung	el **pulmón**
foot	el **pie**
stomach	el **estómago**
dentures	la **dentadura**
ill	**enfermo**

Self-Test 40

dizzy	_____
dentist	_____
weak	_____
filling	_____
heel	_____
lung	_____
foot	_____
stomach	_____
dentures	_____
ill	_____

List 41-1

feverish	con fiebre
to hurt	doler
pills	las píldoras
pregnant	embarazada
medicine	la medicina
sharp	agudo
dull	sordo
heart	el corazón
doctor	un doctor
to take	tomar

List 41-2

sharp	agudo
medicine	la medicina
pregnant	embarazada
heart	el corazón
dull	sordo
pills	las píldoras
doctor	un doctor
to hurt	doler
to take	tomar
feverish	con fiebre

List 41-3

doctor	un doctor
dull	sordo
to take	tomar
medicine	la medicina
to hurt	doler
pregnant	embarazada
feverish	con fiebre
pills	las píldoras
sharp	agudo
heart	el corazón

Self-Test 41

doctor	_____
dull	_____
to take	_____
medicine	_____
to hurt	_____
pregnant	_____
feverish	_____
pills	_____
sharp	_____
heart	_____

Difficulties
Apuros

List 42-1

manager	el **director**
bag	un **bolso**
money	el **dinero**
to lose	**perder**
wallet	la **cartera**
jewelry	las **joyas**
to help	**ayudar**
bracelet	la **pulsera**
everything	**todo**
to steal	**robar**

List 42-2

jewelry	las **joyas**
wallet	la **cartera**
to lose	**perder**
bracelet	la **pulsera**
to help	**ayudar**
money	el **dinero**
everything	**todo**
bag	un **bolso**
to steal	**robar**
manager	el **director**

List 42-3

everything	**todo**
to help	**ayudar**
to steal	**robar**
jewelry	las **joyas**
bag	un **bolso**
to lose	**perder**
manager	el **director**
money	el **dinero**
wallet	la **cartera**
bracelet	la **pulsera**

Self-Test 42

everything	_____
to help	_____
to steal	_____
jewelry	_____
bag	_____
to lose	_____
manager	_____
money	_____
wallet	_____
bracelet	_____

Dialogue 11A

A: Today I lost my camera and bag with everything. Where is the police station?

B: Over there, straight ahead and then to the left of the museum, near the church.

A: Also, I have a pain in my back. It's a sharp pain. Please, where is a doctor?

A: Hoy perdí mi cámara y bolso con todo. ¿Dónde está la comisaría de policía?

B: Allí, todo recto y entonces a la izquierda del museo, cerca de la iglesia.

A: También, me duele la espalda. Es un dolor agudo. Por favor, ¿dónde está un doctor?

Dialogue 11B

A: Please help me. I bought a bracelet on Tuesday. Now I have lost my bracelet and my wallet. Also, someone has stolen my money. I'm ill, I have a headache and need medicine.

B: You must go to the hospital, then to the police station.

A: Por favor ayúdeme. Compré una pulsera el martes. Ahora he perdido mi pulsera y mi cartera. También, alguien ha robado mi dinero. Estoy enferma, tengo dolor de cabeza y necesito medicina.

B: Tiene que ir al hospital, entonces a la comisaría de policía.

Mail
El Correo

List 43-1

letter	la **carta**
stamp	el **sello**
mail	el **correo**
to send	**enviar**
local	**local**
abroad	**al extranjero**
telegram	un **telegrama**
to cash	**cobrar**
to change	**cambiar**
check	el **cheque**

List 43-2

abroad	**al extranjero**
local	**local**
to send	**enviar**
to cash	**cobrar**
telegram	un **telegrama**
mail	el **correo**
to change	**cambiar**
stamp	el **sello**
check	el **cheque**
letter	la **carta**

List 43-3

to change	**cambiar**
telegram	un **telegrama**
check	el **cheque**
abroad	**al extranjero**
stamp	el **sello**
to send	**enviar**
letter	la **carta**
mail	el **correo**
local	**local**
to cash	**cobrar**

Self-Test 43

to change	_____
telegram	_____
check	_____
abroad	_____
stamp	_____
to send	_____
letter	_____
mail	_____
local	_____
to cash	_____

Transportation and Entertainment
Transportación y entretenimiento

List 44-1

car	el **coche**
full	**lleno**
tires	los **neumáticos**
lights	los **faros**
battery	la **batería**
brakes	los **frenos**
oil	el **aceite**
to rent	**alquilar**
to look	**mirar**
to repair	**reparar**

List 44-2

brakes	los **frenos**
battery	la **batería**
lights	los **faros**
to rent	**alquilar**
oil	el **aceite**
tires	los **neumáticos**
to look	**mirar**
full	**lleno**
to repair	**reparar**
car	el **coche**

List 44-3

to look	**mirar**
oil	el **aceite**
to repair	**reparar**
brakes	los **frenos**
full	**lleno**
lights	los **faros**
car	el **coche**
tires	los **neumáticos**
battery	la **batería**
to rent	**alquilar**

Self-Test 44

to look	_____
oil	_____
to repair	_____
brakes	_____
full	_____
lights	_____
car	_____
tires	_____
battery	_____
to rent	_____

List 45-1

train	el **tren**
bus	el **autobús**
stop	la **parada**
boat	el **barco**
platform	el **andén**
timetable	el **horario**
cost	el **coste**
seat	el **asiento**
arrival	la **llegada**
departure	la **salida**

List 45-2

timetable	el **horario**
platform	el **andén**
boat	el **barco**
seat	el **asiento**
cost	el **coste**
stop	la **parada**
arrival	la **llegada**
bus	el **autobús**
departure	la **salida**
train	el **tren**

List 45-3

arrival	la **llegada**
cost	el **coste**
departure	la **salida**
timetable	el **horario**
bus	el **autobús**
boat	el **barco**
train	el **tren**
stop	la **parada**
platform	el **andén**
seat	el **asiento**

Self-Test 45

arrival	_____
cost	_____
departure	_____
timetable	_____
bus	_____
boat	_____
train	_____
stop	_____
platform	_____
seat	_____

List 46-1

concert	el concierto
film	la película
play	la obra
race	la carrera
program	un programa
match	el partido
to start	empezar
theatre	el teatro
lessons	las lecciones
skiing	el esquí

List 46-2

match	el partido
program	un programa
race	la carrera
theatre	el teatro
to start	empezar
play	la obra
lessons	las lecciones
film	la película
skiing	el esquí
concert	el concierto

List 46-3

lessons	las lecciones
to start	empezar
skiing	el esquí
match	el partido
film	la película
race	la carrera
concert	el concierto
play	la obra
program	un programa
theatre	el teatro

Self-Test 46

lessons	_____
to start	_____
skiing	_____
match	_____
film	_____
race	_____
concert	_____
play	_____
program	_____
theatre	_____

Dialogue 12A

A: I'd like to send a letter. Please, where is a mailbox?

B: The mailbox is straight ahead at the traffic light.

A: Can I rent a car here?

B: Yes.

A: Can you write down the daily charge and the cost of insurance? Thank you.

A: Quiero enviar una carta. Por favor, ¿dónde está un buzón?

B: El buzón está todo recto al semáforo.

A: ¿Puedo alquilar un coche aquí?

B: Sí.

A: ¿Puede escribir el precio por día y el precio del seguro? Gracias.

Dialogue 12B

A: Can you help me? Repair my car's brakes; estimate the cost.

B: Yes, the cost is about twenty-two dollars.

A: I'd like to cash this check.

B: I'm sorry, we don't cash checks.

A: At what time does the train arrive?

B: The train arrives at two o'clock.

A: ¿Me puede ayudar? Repara los frenos de mi coche; estima el costo.

B: Sí, el costo es cerca veintidós dólares.

A: Quiero cobrar este cheque.

B: Lo siento, no cobramos cheques.

A: ¿Y a qué hora llega el tren?

B: El tren llega a las dos.

Public Information
Información pública

List 47-1

to enter	entrar
to wait	esperar
to come	venir
to sit	sentar
of course	claro
license	la licencia
elevator	el ascensor
highway	la autopista
toilets	los aseos
detour	el desvío

List 47-2

license	la licencia
of course	claro
to sit	sentar
highway	la autopista
elevator	el ascensor
to come	venir
toilets	los aseos
to wait	esperar
detour	el desvío
to enter	entrar

List 47-3

toilets	los aseos
elevator	el ascensor
detour	el desvío
license	la licencia
to wait	esperar
to sit	sentar
to enter	entrar
to come	venir
of course	claro
highway	la autopista

Self-Test 47

toilets	_____
elevator	_____
detour	_____
license	_____
to wait	_____
to sit	_____
to enter	_____
to come	_____
of course	_____
highway	_____

List 48-1

to believe	creer
to swim	nadar
to park	aparcar
to dance	bailar
to say	decir
sale	la liquidación
adults	los mayores
children	los niños
equipment	el equipo
toll	el peaje

List 48-2

sale	la liquidación
to say	decir
to dance	bailar
children	los niños
adults	los mayores
to park	aparcar
equipment	el equipo
to swim	nadar
toll	el peaje
to believe	creer

List 48-3

equipment	el equipo
adults	los mayores
toll	el peaje
sale	la liquidación
to swim	nadar
to dance	bailar
to believe	creer
to park	aparcar
to say	decir
children	los niños

Self-Test 48

equipment	_____
adults	_____
toll	_____
sale	_____
to swim	_____
to dance	_____
to believe	_____
to park	_____
to say	_____
children	_____

List 49-1

care	el **cuidado**
porter	el **conserje**
push	**empuje**
school	la **escuela**
pedestrian	el **peatón**
danger	el **peligro**
caution	la **precaución**
private	**privado**
to give	**dar**
to feel	**sentir**

List 49-2

danger	el **peligro**
pedestrian	el **peatón**
school	la **escuela**
private	**privado**
caution	la **precaución**
push	**empuje**
to give	**dar**
porter	el **conserje**
to feel	**sentir**
care	el **cuidado**

List 49-3

to give	**dar**
caution	la **precaución**
to feel	**sentir**
danger	el **peligro**
porter	el **conserje**
school	la **escuela**
care	el **cuidado**
push	**empuje**
pedestrian	el **peatón**
private	**privado**

Self-Test 49

to give	_____
caution	_____
to feel	_____
danger	_____
porter	_____
school	_____
care	_____
push	_____
pedestrian	_____
private	_____

List 50-1

noon	el **mediodía**
midnight	la **medianoche**
morning	la **mañana**
afternoon	la **tarde**
yesterday	**ayer**
last	**pasado**
next	**próximo**
first	**primero**
second	**segundo**
third	**tercero**

List 50-2

last	**pasado**
yesterday	**ayer**
afternoon	la **tarde**
first	**primero**
next	**próximo**
morning	la **mañana**
second	**segundo**
midnight	la **medianoche**
third	**tercero**
noon	el **mediodía**

List 50-3

second	**segundo**
next	**próximo**
third	**tercero**
last	**pasado**
midnight	la **medianoche**
afternoon	la **tarde**
noon	el **mediodía**
morning	la **mañana**
yesterday	**ayer**
first	**primero**

Self-Test 50

second	_____
next	_____
third	_____
last	_____
midnight	_____
afternoon	_____
noon	_____
morning	_____
yesterday	_____
first	_____

Dialogue 13A

A: Excuse me please. I'd like to swim. Where does the bus leave for the beach?

B: Here, platform one.

A: When does it leave and when does it arrive at the beach?

B: It leaves at eleven o'clock in the morning and it arrives at noon.

A: Thank you.

A: Perdone, por favor. Quiero nadar. ¿De dónde sale el autobus para ir a la playa?

B: Aquí, andén primero.

A: Por favor ¿a qué hora sale y cuándo llega a la playa?

B: Sale a las once de la mañana y llega al mediodía.

A: Gracias.

Dialogue 13B

A: Excuse me please. Can I park here and look around?

B: Of course, but be careful.

A: May one get a drink and something to eat?

B: I don't think so, I'm sorry.

A: That's okay.

A: Perdone, por favor. ¿Se puede aparcar aquí y mirar alrededor?

B: Claro, pero tenga cuidado.

A: ¿Se puede obtener una bebida y algo de comer?

B: No creo, lo siento.

A: Está bien.

Department Store
Almacén

List 51-1

department	la **sección**
drugstore	la **droguería**
cosmetics	los **cosméticos**
carpets	las **alfombras**
food	la **alimentación**
toys	los **juguetes**
furniture	los **muebles**
stationery	la **papelería**
materials	los **retales**
bookstore	la **librería**

List 51-2

toys	los **juguetes**
food	la **alimentación**
carpets	las **alfombras**
stationery	la **papelería**
furniture	los **muebles**
cosmetics	los **cosméticos**
materials	los **retales**
drugstore	la **droguería**
bookstore	la **librería**
department	la **sección**

List 51-3

materials	los **retales**
furniture	los **muebles**
bookstore	la **librería**
toys	los **juguetes**
drugstore	la **droguería**
carpets	las **alfombras**
department	la **sección**
cosmetics	los **cosméticos**
food	la **alimentación**
stationery	la **papelería**

Self-Test 51

materials	_____
furniture	_____
bookstore	_____
toys	_____
drugstore	_____
carpets	_____
department	_____
cosmetics	_____
food	_____
stationery	_____

List 52-1

basement	el sótano
floor	la planta
underwear	la ropa interior
bras	los sostenes
ties	las corbatas
crockery	la vajilla
drapery	la pañería
notions	la mercería
dry goods	la lencería
complaints	las reclamaciones

List 52-2

crockery	la vajilla
ties	las corbatas
bras	los sostenes
notions	la mercería
drapery	la pañería
underwear	la ropa interior
dry goods	la lencería
floor	la planta
complaints	las reclamaciones
basement	el sótano

List 52-3

dry goods	la lencería
drapery	la pañería
complaints	las reclamaciones
crockery	la vajilla
floor	la planta
bras	los sostenes
basement	el sótano
underwear	la ropa interior
ties	las corbatas
notions	la mercería

Self-Test 52

dry goods	_____
drapery	_____
complaints	_____
crockery	_____
floor	_____
bras	_____
basement	_____
underwear	_____
ties	_____
notions	_____

Dialogue 14A

A: Please, I want to buy some food and some stationery. Where are the departments?

B: Foods are on the second floor, stationery is on the third floor.

A: Also, I want to exchange my ties.

B: Take the elevator to the basement.

A: Por favor, quiero comprar alimentaciones y papelerías. ¿Dónde están las secciones?

B: Alimentaciones están en la planta segunda, papelerías están en la planta tercera.

A: También, quiero cambiar mis corbatas.

B: Tome el ascensor al sótano.

Dialogue 14B

A: I feel dizzy. Please, may one sit here?

B: Yes, do you need medicine?

A: Yes, where is the drugstore? I want to buy some aspirin.

B: The drugstore is on the first floor.

A: Thank you.

B: You're welcome.

A: Me siento mareada. Por favor, ¿se puede sentar aquí?

B: Sí, ¿necesita medicina?

A: Sí, ¿dónde está la droguería? Quiero comprar aspirina.

B: La droguería está en la planta primera.

A: Gracias.

B: De nada.

Transportation
La transportación

List 53-1

airplane	el **avión**
truck	el **camión**
bicycle	la **bicicleta**
motorcycle	la **motocicleta**
ship	el **barco**
taxi	el **taxi**
streetcar	el **tranvía**
subway	el **metro**
yacht	el **yate**
sailboat	el **velero**

List 53-2

taxi	el **taxi**
ship	el **barco**
motorcycle	la **motocicleta**
subway	el **metro**
streetcar	el **tranvía**
bicycle	la **bicicleta**
yacht	el **yate**
truck	el **camión**
sailboat	el **velero**
airplane	el **avión**

List 53-3

yacht	el **yate**
streetcar	el **tranvía**
sailboat	el **velero**
taxi	el **taxi**
truck	el **camión**
motorcycle	la **motocicleta**
airplane	el **avión**
bicycle	la **bicicleta**
ship	el **barco**
subway	el **metro**

Self-Test 53

yacht	_____
streetcar	_____
sailboat	_____
taxi	_____
truck	_____
motorcycle	_____
airplane	_____
bicycle	_____
ship	_____
subway	_____

Weather
El clima

List 54-1

rain	la **lluvia**
snow	la **nieve**
storm	la **tormenta**
wind	el **viento**
cloudy	**nublado**
cold	**frío**
wet	**húmedo**
dusty	**polvoriento**
sunny	**asoleado**
clear	**despejado**

List 54-2

cold	**frío**
cloudy	**nublado**
wind	el **viento**
dusty	**polvoriento**
wet	**húmedo**
storm	la **tormenta**
sunny	**asoleado**
snow	la **nieve**
clear	**despejado**
rain	la **lluvia**

List 54-3

sunny	**asoleado**
wet	**húmedo**
clear	**despejado**
cold	**frío**
snow	la **nieve**
wind	el **viento**
rain	la **lluvia**
storm	la **tormenta**
cloudy	**nublado**
dusty	**polvoriento**

Self-Test 54

sunny	_____
wet	_____
clear	_____
cold	_____
snow	_____
wind	_____
rain	_____
storm	_____
cloudy	_____
dusty	_____

Basic
Básico

List 55-1

trip	el **viaje**
fast	**rápido**
slow	**lento**
in	**en**
family	la **familia**
good	**bueno**
bad	**malo**
really	**realmente**
to	**a**
relatives	los **parientes**

List 55-2

good	**bueno**
family	la **familia**
in	**en**
really	**realmente**
bad	**malo**
slow	**lento**
to	**a**
fast	**rápido**
relatives	los **parientes**
trip	el **viaje**

List 55-3

to	**a**
bad	**malo**
relatives	los **parientes**
good	**bueno**
fast	**rápido**
in	**en**
trip	el **viaje**
slow	**lento**
family	la **familia**
really	**realmente**

Self-Test 55

to	_____
bad	_____
relatives	_____
good	_____
fast	_____
in	_____
trip	_____
slow	_____
family	_____
really	_____

Present Tense of Regular Verbs
Los verbos en tiempo presente

(to take—**tomar**, to eat—**comer**, to live—**vivir**)

List 56-1

I take	tomo
you take	tomas
we take	tomamos
they take	toman
I eat	como
you eat	comes
we eat	comemos
they eat	comen
I live	vivo
you live	vives
we live	vivimos
they live	viven

List 56-2

I eat	como
you eat	come
we eat	comemos
they eat	comen
I live	vivo
you live	vive
we live	vivimos
they live	viven
I take	tomo
you take	toma
we take	tomamos
they take	toman

List 56-3

I live	vivo
you live	vive
we live	vivimos
they live	viven
I take	tomo
you take	toma
we take	tomamos
they take	toman
I eat	como
you eat	come
we eat	comemos
they eat	comen

Self-Test 56

I live	_____
you live	_____
we live	_____
they live	_____
I take	_____
you take	_____
we take	_____
they take	_____
I eat	_____
you eat	_____
we eat	_____
they eat	_____

Dialogue 15A

A: We want to take a trip.

A: Queremos tomar un viaje.

B: Where do you want to go?

B: ¿Adónde quieren ir?

A: Madrid and Seville. I want to visit my family in Madrid and my friend wants to visit her relatives in Seville.

A: Madrid y Sevilla. Quiero visitar a mi familia en Madrid y mi amiga quiere visitar a sus parientes en Sevilla.

B: You take an airplane in the morning to Madrid, then in the afternoon, a slow train to Seville.

B: Toman un avión en la mañana a Madrid, entonces en la tarde, un tren lento a Sevilla.

A: Thank you.

A: Gracias.

B: You're welcome.

B: De nada.

Dialogue 15B

A: We will arrive at eleven o'clock in the morning when the weather is bad— cold, humid, and cloudy. We'll eat and then we'll take a fast taxi to the hotel. But in the afternoon, the weather is good—sunny, warm, and clear. And in the evening we'll have rain.

A: Vamos a llegar a las once de la mañana cuando hace mal tiempo—frío, húmedo y nublado. Vamos a comer y entonces vamos a tomar un taxi rápido al hotel. Pero en la tarde, hace buen tiempo—asoleado, caliente y despejado. Y en la noche vamos a tener lluvia.

Present Tense of Irregular Verbs
Verbos irregulares en tiempo presente

(to hear—**oír**, to make—**hacer**)

List 57-1

to hear	**oír**
I hear	**oigo**
you hear	**oye**
we hear	**oímos**
they hear	**oyen**
to make	**hacer**
I make	**hago**
you make	**haces**
we make	**hacemos**
they make	**hacen**

List 57-2

to make	**hacer**
I make	**hago**
you make	**haces**
we make	**hacemos**
they make	**hacen**
to hear	**oír**
I hear	**oigo**
you hear	**oye**
we hear	**oímos**
they hear	**oyen**

List 57-3

to hear	**oír**
I hear	**oigo**
you hear	**oye**
we hear	**oímos**
they hear	**oyen**
to make	**hacer**
I make	**hago**
you make	**hace**
we make	**hacemos**
they make	**hacen**

Self-Test 57

to hear	_____
I hear	_____
you hear	_____
we hear	_____
they hear	_____
to make	_____
I make	_____
you make	_____
we make	_____
they make	_____

(to be—**estar**, to be—**ser**, to prefer—**preferir**)

List 58-1

I am	**estoy**
you are	**está**
we are	**estamos**
they are	**están**
I am	**soy**
he is	**es**
we are	**somos**
they are	**son**
I prefer	**prefiero**
you prefer	**prefiere**
we prefer	**preferimos**
they prefer	**prefieren**

List 58-2

I am	**soy**
you are	**es**
we are	**somos**
they are	**son**
I prefer	**prefiero**
you prefer	**prefiere**
we prefer	**preferimos**
they prefer	**prefieren**
I am	**estoy**
she is	**está**
we are	**estamos**
they are	**están**

List 58-3

I prefer	**prefiero**
you prefer	**prefiere**
we prefer	**preferimos**
they prefer	**prefieren**
I am	**estoy**
he is	**está**
we are	**estamos**
they are	**están**
I am	**soy**
she is	**es**
we are	**somos**
they are	**son**

Self-Test 58

I prefer	_____
you prefer	_____
we prefer	_____
they prefer	_____
I am	_____
he is	_____
we are	_____
they are	_____
I am	_____
she is	_____
we are	_____
they are	_____

(to think—**pensar**, to know—**saber, conocer**)

List 59-1

I think	**pienso**
you think	**piensa**
we think	**pensamos**
they think	**piensan**
I know	**sé**
you know	**sabe**
we know	**sabemos**
they know	**saben**
I know	**conozco**
you know	**conoce**
we know	**conocemos**
they know	**conocen**

List 59-2

I know	**sé**
you know	**sabes**
we know	**sabemos**
they know	**saben**
I know	**conozco**
you know	**conoce**
we know	**conocemos**
they know	**conocen**
I think	**pienso**
you think	**piensa**
we think	**pensamos**
they think	**piensan**

List 59-3

I know	**conozco**
you know	**conoce**
we know	**conocemos**
they know	**conocen**
I think	**pienso**
you think	**piensa**
we think	**pensamos**
they think	**piensan**
I know	**sé**
you know	**sabe**
we know	**sabemos**
they know	**saben**

Self-Test 59

I know	_____
you know	_____
we know	_____
they know	_____
I think	_____
you think	_____
we think	_____
they think	_____
I know	_____
you know	_____
we know	_____
they know	_____

(to be able—**poder**; other irregular verbs in the first person singular)

List 60-1

I can	puedo
you can	puede
we can	podemos
they can	pueden
to show	mostrar
to put	poner
I put	pongo
I say	digo
I give	doy
I see	veo

List 60-2

I put	pongo
to show	mostrar
I say	digo
I see	veo
I give	doy
I can	puedo
you can	puede
we can	podemos
they can	pueden
to put	poner

List 60-3

I say	digo
to put	poner
I see	veo
I put	pongo
I give	doy
to show	mostrar
I can	puedo
you can	puede
we can	podemos
they can	pueden

Self-Test 60

I say	_____
to put	_____
I see	_____
I put	_____
I give	_____
to show	_____
I can	_____
you can	_____
we can	_____
they can	_____

(to go—ir, to come—venir, to want—querer)

List 61-1

I go	**voy**
you go	**va**
we go	**vamos**
they go	**van**
I come	**vengo**
you come	**viene**
we come	**venimos**
they come	**vienen**
I want	**quiero**
you want	**quiere**
we want	**queremos**
they want	**quieren**

List 61-2

I come	**vengo**
you come	**viene**
we come	**venimos**
they come	**vienen**
I want	**quiero**
you want	**quiere**
we want	**queremos**
they want	**quieren**
I go	**voy**
you go	**va**
we go	**vamos**
they go	**van**

List 61-3

I want	**quiero**
you want	**quiere**
we want	**queremos**
they want	**quieren**
I go	**voy**
you go	**va**
we go	**vamos**
they go	**van**
I come	**vengo**
you come	**viene**
we come	**venimos**
they come	**vienen**

Self-Test 61

I want	_____
you want	_____
we want	_____
they want	_____
I go	_____
you go	_____
we go	_____
they go	_____
I come	_____
you come	_____
we come	_____
they come	_____

Family and Relatives
La familia y los parientes

List 62-1

aunt	la **tía**
uncle	el **tío**
father	el **padre**
mother	la **madre**
brother	el **hermano**
sister	la **hermana**
cousin	el **primo**
grandmother	la **abuela**
grandfather	el **abuelo**
nephew	el **sobrino**

List 62-2

cousin	el **primo**
sister	la **hermana**
grandfather	el **abuelo**
grandmother	la **abuela**
nephew	el **sobrino**
aunt	la **tía**
father	el **padre**
uncle	el **tío**
brother	el **hermano**
mother	la **madre**

List 62-3

father	el **padre**
aunt	la **tía**
brother	el **hermano**
uncle	el **tío**
mother	la **madre**
cousin	el **primo**
grandfather	el **abuelo**
sister	la **hermana**
nephew	el **sobrino**
grandmother	la **abuela**

Self-Test 62

father	_____
aunt	_____
brother	_____
uncle	_____
mother	_____
cousin	_____
grandfather	_____
sister	_____
nephew	_____
grandmother	_____

Dialogue 16A

A: Louis, are you going to call your family?

B: I really prefer to first call my aunt Rose.

A: Good, I know her.

B: Hello, Aunt Rose, I'm your nephew, Louis. How are you?

C: I'm very well, where are you?

B: Here, in Madrid. Are you able to come to my family's house tonight?

C: Of course.

A: Luis, ¿va a hacer una llamada a su familia?

B: Prefiero realmente primero llamar a mi tía Rosa.

A: Bueno, la conozco.

B: Hola, tía Rosa, soy su sobrino, Luis. ¿Cómo está usted?

C: Estoy muy bien, ¿dónde estás?

B: Aquí, en Madrid. ¿Puede venir a la casa de mi familia esta noche?

C: Claro.

Dialogue 16B

A: What is the address of your family's house?

B: They live at number seventeen on John Street. Do you want to come with me to see them?

A: Yes, of course, I want to meet your mother, father, and brother. When do you want to go, tonight or Saturday? Let's go now.

B: No, we'll go tonight.

A: ¿Cuál es la dirección de la casa de su familia?

B: Viven en número diez y siete en la calle San Juan. ¿Quiere venir conmigo a verlos?

A: Sí, claro, que quiero conocer a su madre, padre y hermano. ¿Cuándo quiere ir, esta noche o sábado? Vamos ahora.

B: No, vamos a ir esta noche

Basic
Básico

List 63-1

friend	un **amigo**
people	la **gente**
now	**ahora**
by	**por**
happy	**feliz**
sad	**triste**
out, outside	**fuera**
call	una **llamada**
up	**arriba**
down	**abajo**

List 63-2

out, outside	**fuera**
sad	**triste**
up	**arriba**
call	una **llamada**
down	**abajo**
friend	un **amigo**
now	**ahora**
people	la **gente**
happy	**feliz**
by	**por**

List 63-3

now	**ahora**
friend	un **amigo**
happy	**feliz**
people	la **gente**
by	**por**
out, outside	**fuera**
up	**arriba**
sad	**triste**
down	**abajo**
call	una **llamada**

Self-Test 63

now	_____
friend	_____
happy	_____
people	_____
by	_____
out, outside	_____
up	_____
sad	_____
down	_____
call	_____

Parts of a House
Las partes de la casa

List 64-1

closet	un **ropero**
bedroom	una **alcoba**
living room	una **sala**
dining room	el **comedor**
room	un **cuarto**
floor	el **piso**
window	la **ventana**
door	la **puerta**
hall	el **pasillo**
stairway	la **escalera**

List 64-2

window	la **ventana**
floor	el **piso**
hall	el **pasillo**
door	la **puerta**
stairway	la **escalera**
closet	un **ropero**
living room	una **sala**
bedroom	una **alcoba**
room	un **cuarto**
dining room	el **comedor**

List 64-3

living room	una **sala**
closet	un **ropero**
room	un **cuarto**
bedroom	una **alcoba**
dining room	el **comedor**
window	la **ventana**
hall	el **pasillo**
floor	el **piso**
stairway	la **escalera**
door	la **puerta**

Self-Test 64

living room	_____
closet	_____
room	_____
bedroom	_____
dining room	_____
window	_____
hall	_____
floor	_____
stairway	_____
door	_____

Dialogue 17A

A: It's eight o'clock at night and it's raining. We need raincoats. First we take a streetcar and then the subway that goes to John Street. Now we are at my family's house and I knock on the door. My grandmother opens the door and we enter. I see my mother and father sitting in the living room.

A: Son las ocho de la noche y está lloviendo. Necesitamos impermeables. Primero tomamos un tranvía y entonces el metro que va a la calle San Juan. Ahora estamos en la casa de mi familia y llamo a la puerta. Mi abuela abre la puerta y entramos. Veo mi madre y padre sentados en la sala.

Dialogue 17B

A: Louis, I am very happy that you are here, and who is the young lady?

B: I introduce my friend Anne. Anne, Julia my mother.

C: Delighted to meet you.

B: Where is Arthur?

A: Your brother is away this week, but your aunt Rose and cousin John are waiting in the dining room for dinner.

A: Luis, estoy muy feliz que está aquí, ¿y quién es la señorita?

B: Le presento a mi amiga Anne. Anne, Julia, mi madre.

C: Encantado.

B: ¿Dónde está Arturo?

A: Tu hermano está fuera esta semana, pero tu tía Rosa y primo Juan están esperando en el comedor para la cena.

Dwellings and Furniture
Las moradas y los muebles

List 65-1

apartment	un **apartamento**
hotel	un **hotel**
cottage	una **caseta**
farmhouse	una **alquería**
chair	una **silla**
table	una **mesa**
mirror	un **espejo**
lamp	una **lámpara**
couch	un **sofá**
dresser	una **cómoda**

List 65-2

mirror	un **espejo**
table	una **mesa**
couch	un **sofá**
lamp	una **lámpara**
dresser	una **cómoda**
apartment	un **apartamento**
cottage	una **caseta**
hotel	un **hotel**
chair	una **silla**
farmhouse	una **alquería**

List 65-3

cottage	una **caseta**
apartment	un **apartamento**
chair	una **silla**
hotel	un **hotel**
farmhouse	una **alquería**
mirror	un **espejo**
couch	un **sofá**
table	una **mesa**
dresser	una **cómoda**
lamp	una **lámpara**

Self 65

cottage	_____
apartment	_____
chair	_____
hotel	_____
farmhouse	_____
mirror	_____
couch	_____
table	_____
dresser	_____
lamp	_____

Present Tense of Irregular Verbs
Verbos irregulares en tiempo presente

(to have—**tener**, to bring—**traer**)

List 66-1

I have	**tengo**
you have	**tiene**
we have	**tenemos**
they have	**tienen**
to keep	**retener**
to bring	**traer**
I bring	**traigo**
you bring	**trae**
we bring	**traemos**
they bring	**traen**

List 66-2

to keep	**retener**
to bring	**traer**
I bring	**traigo**
you bring	**trae**
we bring	**traemos**
they bring	**traen**
I have	**tengo**
you have	**tiene**
we have	**tenemos**
they have	**tienen**

List 66-3

I bring	**traigo**
you bring	**trae**
we bring	**traemos**
they bring	**traen**
I have	**tengo**
you have	**tiene**
we have	**tenemos**
they have	**tienen**
to bring	**traer**
to keep	**retener**

Self-Test 66

I bring	_____
you bring	_____
we bring	_____
they bring	_____
I have	_____
you have	_____
we have	_____
they have	_____
to bring	_____
to keep	_____

Review Test 2

List	Test Words	Answer
34	oranges	_____
	cherries	_____
35	beef	_____
	steak	_____
36	shrimp	_____
	sole	_____
37	milk shake	_____
	cider	_____
38	sweet	_____
	dry	_____
39	ear	_____
	eye	_____
40	foot	_____
	stomach	_____
41	dull	_____
	sharp	_____
42	to help	_____
	wallet	_____
43	stamp	_____
	mail	_____
44	car	_____
	to rent	_____
45	departure	_____
	arrival	_____
46	film	_____
	concert	_____

List	Test Words	Answer (continued)
47	highway	_____
	detour	_____
48	adults	_____
	children	_____
49	porter	_____
	school	_____
50	afternoon	_____
	yesterday	_____
51	toys	_____
	bookstore	_____
52	complaints	_____
	underwear	_____
53	truck	_____
	streetcar	_____
54	clear	_____
	rain	_____
55	really	_____
	trip	_____
56	I live	_____
	they eat	_____
57	you hear	_____
	we make	_____
58	I prefer	_____
	they are	_____
59	we think	_____
	I know	_____
60	he can	_____
	I put	_____

List	Test Words	Answer (continued)
61	they go	_____
	she wants	_____
62	sister	_____
	nephew	_____
63	people	_____
	now	_____
64	closet	_____
	stairway	_____
65	chair	_____
	couch	_____
66	we have	_____
	to bring	_____

CD 3

Dialogue 18A

A: Louis, please leave the hotel and come here. We have three bedrooms. You can sleep in the room downstairs, and your friend Anne in the bedroom upstairs, to the right of the stairs.

B: Is there a closet for Anne?

A: Yes, and also there is a chair, a window, and in the dresser there is a mirror.

B: Great! I know she'll like it.

A: Luis, por favor sale del hotel y venga aquí. Tenemos tres alcobas. Puede dormir en el cuarto abajo, y su amiga Anne en la alcoba arriba, a la derecha de la escalera.

B: ¿Hay un ropero para Anne?

A: Sí, también una silla, una ventana, y en la cómoda hay un espejo.

B: ¡Estupendo! Sé que le va a gustar.

Dialogue 18B

A: Anne, I'm hungry. Would you like to come with me to my favorite restaurant?

B: Yes, but I have to follow a special diet. My food cannot have fat.

A: Good, do you like salad?

B: Yes, but I only like lettuce and tomatoes with radishes, cucumbers, onions, and celery.

A: Let's go.

A: Anne, tengo hambre. ¿Quiere venir conmigo a mi restaurante favorito?

B: Sí, pero debo seguir una dieta especial. Mi comida no puede tener grasa.

A: Bueno, ¿le gusta la ensalada?

B: Sí, pero solamente me gusta lechuga y tomates con rábanos, pepinos, cebollas y apio.

A: Vamos.

Beverages
Las bebidas

List 67-1

wine	un **vino**
vodka	una **vodka**
bourbon	un **borbón**
scotch	el **whisky escocés**
champagne	una **champaña**
juice	un **jugo**
tea	un **té**
punch	un **ponche**
orangeade	una **naranjada**
soda	una **soda**

List 67-2

tea	un **té**
juice	un **jugo**
orangeade	una **naranjada**
punch	un **ponche**
soda	una **soda**
wine	un **vino**
bourbon	un **borbón**
vodka	una **vodka**
champagne	una **champaña**
scotch	el **whisky escocés**

List 67-3

bourbon	un **borbón**
wine	un **vino**
champagne	una **champaña**
vodka	una **vodka**
scotch	el **whisky escocés**
tea	un **té**
orangeade	una **naranjada**
juice	un **jugo**
soda	una **soda**
punch	un **ponche**

Self-Test 67

bourbon	_____
wine	_____
champagne	_____
vodka	_____
scotch	_____
tea	_____
orangeade	_____
juice	_____
soda	_____
punch	_____

Food and Cooking
El alimento y la cocina

List 68-1

favorite	favorito
fat	la grasa
diet	una dieta
roasted	asado
broiled	a la parrilla
fried	frito
steamed	al vapor
sauce	la salsa
salad	una ensalada
dessert	un postre

List 68-2

steamed	al vapor
fried	frito
salad	una ensalada
sauce	la salsa
dessert	un postre
favorite	favorito
diet	una dieta
fat	la grasa
broiled	a la parrilla
roasted	asado

List 68-3

diet	una dieta
favorite	favorito
broiled	a la parrilla
fat	la grasa
roasted	asado
steamed	al vapor
salad	una ensalada
fried	frito
dessert	un postre
sauce	la salsa

Self-Test 68

diet	_____
favorite	_____
broiled	_____
fat	_____
roasted	_____
steamed	_____
salad	_____
fried	_____
dessert	_____
sauce	_____

List 69-1

barbecued	a la barbacoa
stew	un estofado
poached	escalfado
baked	horneado
boiled	hervido
fresh	fresco
sautéed	salteado
toasted	tostado
smoked	ahumado
raw	crudo

List 69-2

sautéed	salteado
fresh	fresco
smoked	ahumado
toasted	tostado
raw	crudo
barbecued	a la barbacoa
poached	escalfado
stew	un estofado
boiled	hervido
baked	horneado

List 69-3

poached	escalfado
barbecued	a la barbacoa
boiled	hervido
stew	un estofado
baked	horneado
sautéed	salteado
smoked	ahumado
fresh	fresco
raw	crudo
toasted	tostado

Self-Test 69

poached	_____
barbecued	_____
boiled	_____
stew	_____
baked	_____
sautéed	_____
smoked	_____
fresh	_____
raw	_____
toasted	_____

List 70-1

pan	la **cazuela**
pot	el **pote**
bowl	el **cuenco**
pepper	la **pimienta**
garlic	el **ajo**
spice	la **especia**
mustard	la **mostaza**
lemon	el **limón**
pineapple	la **piña**
cinnamon	la **canela**

List 70-2

mustard	la **mostaza**
spice	la **especia**
pineapple	la **piña**
lemon	el **limón**
cinnamon	la **canela**
pan	la **cazuela**
bowl	el **cuenco**
pot	el **pote**
garlic	el **ajo**
pepper	la **pimienta**

List 70-3

bowl	el **cuenco**
pan	la **cazuela**
garlic	el **ajo**
pot	el **pote**
pepper	la **pimienta**
mustard	la **mostaza**
pineapple	la **piña**
spice	la **especia**
cinnamon	la **canela**
lemon	el **limón**

Self-Test 70

bowl	_____
pan	_____
garlic	_____
pot	_____
pepper	_____
mustard	_____
pineapple	_____
spice	_____
cinnamon	_____
lemon	_____

Vegetables
Las legumbres

List 71-1

celery	el apio
cabbage	el repollo
beets	las remolachas
onion	la cebolla
rice	el arroz
cucumber	el pepino
radishes	los rábanos
squash	la calabaza
cauliflower	la coliflor
mushrooms	los champiñones

List 71-2

radishes	los rábanos
cucumber	el pepino
cauliflower	la coliflor
squash	la calabaza
mushrooms	los champiñones
celery	el apio
beets	las remolachas
cabbage	el repollo
rice	el arroz
onion	la cebolla

List 71-3

beets	las remolachas
celery	el apio
rice	el arroz
cabbage	el repollo
onion	la cebolla
radishes	los rábanos
cauliflower	la coliflor
cucumber	el pepino
mushrooms	los champiñones
squash	la calabaza

Self-Test 71

beets	_____
celery	_____
rice	_____
cabbage	_____
onion	_____
radishes	_____
cauliflower	_____
cucumber	_____
mushrooms	_____
squash	_____

Basic
Básico

List 72-1

too much	**demasiado**
thirst	la **sed**
hunger	la **hambre**
dream	el **sueño**
only	**solo**
to sleep	**dormir**
to get up	**levantarse**
before	**antes**
after	**después de**
to find	**hallar**

List 72-2

to get up	**levantarse**
to sleep	**dormir**
after	**después de**
before	**antes**
to find	**hallar**
too much	**demasiado**
hunger	la **hambre**
thirst	la **sed**
only	**solo**
dream	el **sueño**

List 72-3

hunger	la **hambre**
too much	**demasiado**
only	**solo**
thirst	la **sed**
dream	el **sueño**
to get up	**levantarse**
after	**después de**
to sleep	**dormir**
to find	**hallar**
before	**antes**

Self-Test 72

hunger	_____
too much	_____
only	_____
thirst	_____
dream	_____
to get up	_____
after	_____
to sleep	_____
to find	_____
before	_____

Dialogue 19A

A: Louis, before I woke up, I had a dream.

B: What did you dream?

A: We were hot, you drank wine and I drank juice, but we didn't drink water. What does it mean?

B: Anne, it's easy, it means that you love me or maybe that you have to follow a special diet.

A: I'm going to sleep, maybe I'll dream another dream.

A: Luis, antes que me levanté, tuve un sueño.

B: ¿Qué soñó?

A: Tuvimos calor, Ud. bebió vino, y yo bebí jugo, pero no bebimos agua. ¿Qué significa?

B: Anne, es fácil, significa que me ama o quizás que debe seguir una dieta especial.

A: Voy a dormir, quizás voy a soñar otro sueño.

Dialogue 19B

A: Anne, I found a store that has seasonings for your salads.

B: Where?

A: On Prince Street. They have pepper and garlic, also many sauces.

B: When can we go?

A: Today, this afternoon after we visit the museum.

B: Great! I'll like it a lot.

A: Now let's go to the museum.

A: Anne, hallé una tienda que tiene condimentos para sus ensaladas.

B: ¿Adónde?

A: En la calle Príncipe. Tienen pimienta y ajo, también muchas salsas.

B: ¿Cuándo podemos ir?

A: Hoy, esta tarde después que visitemos al museo.

B: ¡Estupendo! me va gustar mucho.

A: Ahora, vamos al museo.

List 73-1

to listen	escuchar
to read	leer
to walk	andar
to run	correr
whom (who)	quien
other	otro
which?	¿cuál?
very	muy
without	sin
with you	contigo

List 73-2

which?	¿cuál?
other	otro
without	sin
very	muy
with you	contigo
to listen	escuchar
to walk	andar
to read	leer
whom (who)	quien
to run	correr

List 73-3

to walk	andar
to listen	escuchar
whom (who)	quien
to read	leer
to run	correr
which?	¿cuál?
without	sin
other	otro
with you	contigo
very	muy

Self-Test 73

to walk	_____
to listen	_____
whom (who)	_____
to read	_____
to run	_____
which?	_____
without	_____
other	_____
with you	_____
very	_____

Rest and Relaxation
Descanse y la relajación

List 74-1

fishing	la **pesca**
magazine	la **revista**
book	el **libro**
novel	la **novela**
article	el **artículo**
library	la **biblioteca**
sports	los **deportes**
soccer	el **balompié**
bullfight	la **corrida de toros**
swim	una **nadada**

List 74-2

sports	los **deportes**
library	la **biblioteca**
bullfight	la **corrida de toros**
soccer	el **balompié**
swim	una **nadada**
fishing	la **pesca**
book	el **libro**
magazine	la **revista**
article	el **artículo**
novel	la **novela**

List 74-3

book	el **libro**
fishing	la **pesca**
article	el **artículo**
magazine	la **revista**
novel	la **novela**
sports	los **deportes**
bullfight	la **corrida de toros**
library	la **biblioteca**
swim	una **nadada**
soccer	el **balompié**

Self-Test 74

book	_____
fishing	_____
article	_____
magazine	_____
novel	_____
sports	_____
bullfight	_____
library	_____
swim	_____
soccer	_____

Music
La música

List 75-1

piano	un **piano**
drum	un **tambor**
violin	un **violín**
clarinet	un **clarinete**
guitar	una **guitarra**
jazz	el **jazz**
classical	**clásico**
music	la **música**
symphony	la **sinfonía**
song	la **canción**

List 75-2

classical	**clásico**
jazz	el **jazz**
symphony	la **sinfonía**
music	la **música**
song	la **canción**
piano	un **piano**
violin	un **violín**
drum	un **tambor**
guitar	una **guitarra**
clarinet	un **clarinete**

List 75-3

violin	un **violín**
piano	un **piano**
guitar	una **guitarra**
drum	un **tambor**
clarinet	un **clarinete**
classical	**clásico**
symphony	la **sinfonía**
jazz	el **jazz**
song	la **canción**
music	la **música**

Self-Test 75

violin	_____
piano	_____
guitar	_____
drum	_____
clarinet	_____
classical	_____
symphony	_____
jazz	_____
song	_____
music	_____

Verbs in the Past Tense
Los verbos en tiempo pasado

(to buy—**comprar**, to eat—**comer**, to say—**decir**)

List 76-1

I bought	**compré**
you bought	**compró**
we bought	**compramos**
they bought	**compraron**
I ate	**comí**
you ate	**comió**
we ate	**comimos**
they ate	**comieron**
I said	**dije**
I spoke	**hablé**

List 76-2

I ate	**comí**
you ate	**comió**
we ate	**comimos**
they ate	**comieron**
I said	**dije**
I spoke	**hablé**
I bought	**compré**
you bought	**compró**
we bought	**compramos**
they bought	**compraron**

List 76-3

I said	**dije**
I spoke	**hablé**
I bought	**compré**
you bought	**compró**
we bought	**compramos**
they bought	**compraron**
I ate	**comí**
you ate	**comió**
we ate	**comimos**
they ate	**comieron**

Self-Test 76

I said	_____
I spoke	_____
I bought	_____
you bought	_____
we bought	_____
they bought	_____
I ate	_____
you ate	_____
we ate	_____
they ate	_____

(to be able—**poder**, to have—**tener**, to want—**querer**)

List 77-1

I could	**pude**
you could	**pudo** *pudiste*
He we could	**pudimos** *pud*
they could	**pudieron**
I had	**tuve**
~~you~~ had	**tuvo**
we had	**tuvimos**
they had	**tuvieron**
I wanted	**quise**
~~you~~ wanted	**quiso**
we wanted	**quisimos**
they wanted	**quisieron**

List 77-2

I had	**tuve**
~~you~~ had	**tuvo**
we had	**tuvimos**
they had	**tuvieron**
I wanted	**quise**
~~you~~ wanted	**quiso**
we wanted	**quisimos**
they wanted	**quisieron**
I could	**pude**
~~you~~ could	**pudo**
we could	**pudimos**
they could	**pudieron**

List 77-3

I wanted	**quise**
~~you~~ wanted	**quiso**
we wanted	**quisimos**
they wanted	**quisieron**
I could	**pude**
~~you~~ could	**pudo**
we could	**pudimos**
they could	**pudieron**
I had	**tuve**
~~you~~ had	**tuvo**
we had	**tuvimos**
they had	**tuvieron**

Self-Test 77

I wanted	_____
He ~~you~~ wanted	_____
we wanted	_____
they wanted	_____
I could	_____
~~you~~ could	_____
we could	_____
they could	_____
I had	_____
~~you~~ had	_____
we had	_____
they had	_____

Dialogue 20A

A: Yesterday I wanted to go to the library, but I had a fever.

B: Anne, I wanted to go fishing but I couldn't because I had an inflamed muscle.

A: Today we're well, let's go to a movie.

A: **Ayer quise ir a la biblioteca, pero tuve una calentura.**

B: **Anne, yo quise ir a pescar pero no pude porque tuve un músculo inflamado.**

A: **Hoy estamos bien, vamos al cine.**

Dialogue 20B

A: Louis, we are going to leave on Friday, what are you going to do on Thursday?

B: In the morning, I'm going to buy some gifts for my family and your relatives. In the afternoon, I'm going to see the bullfight. And in the evening, what do you want to do?

A: I'm going to go to a concert; I like to listen to classical music of the symphony.

A: **Luis, nos vamos a ir el viernes, ¿qué va a hacer el jueves?**

B: **Por la mañana, voy a comprar unos regalos para mi familia y sus parientes. Por la tarde, voy a ver la corrida de toros. Y por la noche, ¿qué va a querer hacer?**

A: **Voy a ir al concierto; me gusta escuchar música clásica de la sinfonía.**

(to go—ir, to be—ser, to be—estar, to put—poner, to give—dar)

List 78-1

I went	fui
you went	fue
we went	fuimos
they went	fueron
I put	puse
I gave	di
I was	estuve
you were	estuvo
we were	estuvimos
they were	estuvieron

List 78-2

I put	puse
I gave	di
I was	estuve
you were	estuvo
we were	estuvimos
they were	estuvieron
I went	fui
you went	fue
we went	fuimos
they went	fueron

List 78-3

I was	estuve
you were	estuvo
we were	estuvimos
they were	estuvieron
I went	fui
you went	fue
we went	fuimos
they went	fueron
I put	puse
I gave	di

Self-Test 78

I was	_____
you were	_____
we were	_____
they were	_____
I went	_____
you went	_____
we went	_____
they went	_____
I put	_____
I gave	_____

(to come—**venir**, to fall—**caer**, to make—**hacer**)

List 79-1

I came	vine
you came	vino
we came	vinimos
they came	vinieron
I saw	vi
I fell	caí
I made	hice
you made	hizo
we made	hicimos
they made	hicieron

List 79-2

I fell	caí
I saw	vi
I made	hice
you made	hizo
we made	hicimos
they made	hicieron
I came	vine
you came	vino
we came	vinimos
they came	vinieron

List 79-3

I made	hice
you made	hizo
we made	hicimos
they made	hicieron
I came	vine
you came	vino
we came	vinimos
they came	vinieron
I fell	caí
I saw	vi

Self-Test 79

I made	_____
you made	_____
we made	_____
they made	_____
I came	_____
you came	_____
we came	_____
they came	_____
I fell	_____
I saw	_____

Basic
Básico

List 80-1

expensive	caro
walk	un paseo
into	adentro
than	que
several	varios
maybe	quizás
some	alguno
same	mismo
again	otra vez
line	la línea

List 80-2

some	alguno
maybe	quizás
again	otra vez
same	mismo
line	la línea
expensive	caro
into	adentro
walk	un paseo
several	varios
than	que

List 80-3

into	adentro
expensive	caro
several	varios
walk	un paseo
than	que
some	alguno
again	otra vez
maybe	quizás
line	la línea
same	mismo

Self-Test 80

into	_____
expensive	_____
several	_____
walk	_____
than	_____
some	_____
again	_____
maybe	_____
line	_____
same	_____

Dialogue 21A

A: I was very sad when we left my family, but now I am with you and I feel very happy.

B: Louis, I really wanted to visit your family longer than a week, but I also want to visit my relatives.

A: I understand, thanks.

B: Now, I'm also very happy, but I'm hungry, let's go to the new restaurant.

A: Estuve muy triste cuando dejamos a mi familia, pero ahora estoy contigo y me siento muy feliz.

B: Luis, realmente quise visitar a su familia más de una semana, pero también quiero visitar a mis parientes.

A: Comprendo, gracias.

B: Ahora yo también estoy muy feliz, pero tengo hambre, vamos al nuevo restaurante.

Dialogue 21B

A: Do you have the suitcases?

B: Yes, I have them.

A: And the gifts?

B: Yes, I have them too. I put the brooch, the watch, the earrings, and the scarf for my relatives inside each suitcase, and the other gifts—the dress, the bracelet, the cap, and the novels for your family, I gave to them.

A: ¿Tiene las maletas?

B: Sí, las tengo.

A: ¿Y los regalos?

B: Sí, los tengo también. Puse el broche, el reloj, los aretes y la bufanda para mis parientes adentro de cada maleta, y los otros regalos—el vestido, la pulsera, el gorro y las novelas para su familia, se los di.

Clothing and Fabrics
La ropa y las telas

List 81-1

slip	las enaguas
scarf	la bufanda
slippers	las zapatillas
sweater	el suéter
handkerchief	el pañuelo
silk	la seda
rayon	el rayón
linen	el lino
corduroy	la pana
flannel	la franela

List 81-2

rayon	el rayón
silk	la seda
corduroy	la pana
linen	el lino
flannel	la franela
slip	las enaguas
slippers	las zapatillas
scarf	la bufanda
handkerchief	el pañuelo
sweater	el suéter

List 81-3

slippers	las zapatillas
slip	las enaguas
handkerchief	el pañuelo
scarf	la bufanda
sweater	el suéter
rayon	el rayón
corduroy	la pana
silk	la seda
flannel	la franela
linen	el lino

Self-Test 81

slippers	_____
slip	_____
handkerchief	_____
scarf	_____
sweater	_____
rayon	_____
corduroy	_____
silk	_____
flannel	_____
linen	_____

Dialogue 22A

A: Louis, I know Seville, it has atmosphere, we're going to see Serpent Street. There's a store with beautiful jewelry and I want to buy a pin for my mother.

B: Good, I'm going to buy a ring or maybe a gold watch.

A: Luis, conozco Sevilla, hay ambiente, vamos a ver la calle Sierpes. Hay una tienda de las joyas lindas y quiero comprar un broche para mi madre.

B: Bueno. Voy a comprar un anillo o quizás un reloj de oro.

Dialogue 22B

A: Today we're going to see my relatives. Do you have the gifts?

B: Yes, here is the scarf for your cousin, the silk and the linen for your aunt, also the sweater and the ties for your uncle and something for you.

A: For me, what?

B: Look—gold earrings.

A: I like them but they're very expensive.

A: Hoy vamos a ver mis parientes. ¿Tiene los regalos?

B: Sí, aquí está la bufanda para su prima, la seda y el lino para su tía, también el suéter y las corbatas para su tío, y algo para usted.

A: ¿Para mí, qué?

B: Mira—aretes de oro.

A: Me gustan, pero son muy caros.

Jewelry
Las joyas

List 82-1

diamond	un **diamante**
ruby	un **rubí**
emerald	una **esmeralda**
gold	el **oro**
silver	la **plata**
ring	un **anillo**
necklace	un **collar**
earrings	unos **aretes**
pin	un **alfiler**
watch	un **reloj**

List 82-2

necklace	un **collar**
ring	un **anillo**
pin	un **alfiler**
earrings	unos **aretes**
watch	un **reloj**
diamond	un **diamante**
emerald	una **esmeralda**
ruby	un **rubí**
silver	la **plata**
gold	el **oro**

List 82-3

emerald	una **esmeralda**
diamond	un **diamante**
silver	la **plata**
ruby	un **rubí**
gold	el **oro**
necklace	un **collar**
pin	un **alfiler**
ring	un **anillo**
watch	un **reloj**
earrings	unos **aretes**

Self-Test 82

emerald	_____
diamond	_____
silver	_____
ruby	_____
gold	_____
necklace	_____
pin	_____
ring	_____
watch	_____
earrings	_____

Parts of the Human Body
Las partes del cuerpo humano

List 83-1

hair	el **pelo**
nose	la **nariz**
face	la **cara**
mouth	la **boca**
tooth	el **diente**
tongue	la **lengua**
lips	los **labios**
skin	el **cutis**
blood	la **sangre**
bone	el **hueso**

List 83-2

lips	los **labios**
tongue	la **lengua**
blood	la **sangre**
skin	el **cutis**
bone	el **hueso**
hair	el **pelo**
face	la **cara**
nose	la **nariz**
tooth	el **diente**
mouth	la **boca**

List 83-3

face	la **cara**
hair	el **pelo**
tooth	el **diente**
nose	la **nariz**
mouth	la **boca**
lips	los **labios**
blood	la **sangre**
tongue	la **lengua**
bone	el **hueso**
skin	el **cutis**

Self-Test 83

face	_____
hair	_____
tooth	_____
nose	_____
mouth	_____
lips	_____
blood	_____
tongue	_____
bone	_____
skin	_____

List 84-1

elbow	el codo
abdomen	el abdomen
hand	la mano
finger	el dedo
knee	la rodilla
ankle	el tobillo
kidney	el riñón
chest	el pecho
muscle	el músculo
fingernail	la uña

List 84-2

kidney	el riñón
ankle	el tobillo
muscle	el músculo
chest	el pecho
fingernail	la uña
elbow	el codo
hand	la mano
abdomen	el abdomen
knee	la rodilla
finger	el dedo

List 84-3

hand	la mano
elbow	el codo
knee	la rodilla
abdomen	el abdomen
finger	el dedo
kidney	el riñón
muscle	el músculo
ankle	el tobillo
fingernail	la uña
chest	el pecho

Self-Test 84

hand	_____
elbow	_____
knee	_____
abdomen	_____
finger	_____
kidney	_____
muscle	_____
ankle	_____
fingernail	_____
chest	_____

Illness
Las enfermedades

List 85-1

cancer	el cáncer
measles	el sarampión
pneumonia	la pulmonía
blister	una ampolla
injured	lastimado
inflamed	inflamado
painful	dolorido
fever	una calentura
wound	la herida
allergic	alérgico

List 85-2

painful	dolorido
inflamed	inflamado
wound	la herida
fever	una calentura
allergic	alérgico
cancer	el cáncer
pneumonia	la pulmonía
measles	el sarampión
injured	lastimado
blister	una ampolla

List 85-3

pneumonia	la pulmonía
cancer	el cáncer
injured	lastimado
measles	el sarampión
blister	una ampolla
painful	dolorido
wound	la herida
inflamed	inflamado
allergic	alérgico
fever	una calentura

Self-Test 85

pneumonia	_____
cancer	_____
injured	_____
measles	_____
blister	_____
painful	_____
wound	_____
inflamed	_____
allergic	_____
fever	_____

Dialogue 23A

A: Anne, you know that I must run.
B: Okay, be careful. How long are you going to run?

A: Perhaps forty or fifty minutes.
B: And where?
A: You know, around the park by the church, near the library.
B: Very well, I'll wait.

Dialogue 23B

A: What's the matter?
B: I think my leg is injured.

A: Which one?

B: The right, it hurts a lot. It's a nagging pain.

A: Where?
B: By the ankle and heel.
A: Show it to me.
B: There are no blisters, I think it's a sprain with an inflamed muscle.
A: I'm going to call a taxi, we'll go to the hospital.
B: No, I'll go tomorrow.

A: Anne, sabe que debo correr.
B: Bueno, tenga cuidado. ¿Cuánto tiempo va a correr?

A: Quizás cuarenta o cincuenta minutos.
B: ¿Y dónde?
A: Usted sabe, alrededor del parque por la iglesia cerca de la biblioteca.
B: Muy bien, voy a esperar.

A: ¿Qué pasa?
B: Pienso que mi pierna está lastimada.

A: ¿Cuál?

B: La derecha, me duele mucho. Es un dolor continuo.

A: ¿Dónde?
B: Por el tobillo y el talón.
A: Me lo muestra.
B: No hay ampollas, pienso que es una torcedura con un músculo inflamado.
A: Voy a llamar un taxi, vamos a ir al hospital.
B: No, yo voy a ir mañana.

Adjectives
Los adjetivos

List 86-1

long	**largo**
short	**corto**
dirty	**sucio**
clean	**limpio**
pretty	**lindo**
ugly	**feo**
hard	**duro**
soft	**blando**
new	**nuevo**
old	**viejo**

List 86-2

hard	**duro**
ugly	**feo**
new	**nuevo**
soft	**blando**
old	**viejo**
long	**largo**
dirty	**sucio**
short	**corto**
pretty	**lindo**
clean	**limpio**

List 86-3

dirty	**sucio**
long	**largo**
pretty	**lindo**
short	**corto**
clean	**limpio**
hard	**duro**
new	**nuevo**
ugly	**feo**
old	**viejo**
soft	**blando**

Self-Test 86

dirty	_____
long	_____
pretty	_____
short	_____
clean	_____
hard	_____
new	_____
ugly	_____
old	_____
soft	_____

Basic
Básico

List 87-1

as	**como**
during	**durante**
or	**o**
company	una **compañía**
job	un **empleo**
man	un **hombre**
thing	una **cosa**
why?	**¿por qué?**
because	**porque**
part	una **parte**

List 87-2

thing	una **cosa**
man	un **hombre**
because	**porque**
why?	**¿por qué?**
part	una **parte**
as	**como**
or	**o**
during	**durante**
job	un **empleo**
company	una **compañía**

List 87-3

or	**o**
as	**como**
job	un **empleo**
during	**durante**
company	una **compañía**
thing	una **cosa**
because	**porque**
man	un **hombre**
part	una **parte**
why?	**¿por qué?**

Self-Test 87

or	_____
as	_____
job	_____
during	_____
company	_____
thing	_____
because	_____
man	_____
part	_____
why?	_____

Verbs
Los verbos

List 88-1

to try	tratar
to love	amar
to use	usar
to work	trabajar
to request	pedir
to sell	vender
to ask	preguntar
to answer	contestar
to learn	aprender
to teach	enseñar

List 88-2

to ask	preguntar
to sell	vender
to learn	aprender
to answer	contestar
to teach	enseñar
to try	tratar
to use	usar
to love	amar
to request	pedir
to work	trabajar

List 88-3

to use	usar
to try	tratar
to request	pedir
to love	amar
to work	trabajar
to ask	preguntar
to learn	aprender
to sell	vender
to teach	enseñar
to answer	contestar

Self-Test 88

to use	_____
to try	_____
to request	_____
to love	_____
to work	_____
to ask	_____
to learn	_____
to sell	_____
to teach	_____
to answer	_____

Occupations and Professions
Las ocupaciones y las profesiones

List 89-1

salesman	el **vendedor**
clerk	el **dependiente**
laborer	el **trabajador**
merchant	el **comerciante**
mechanic	el **mecánico**
lawyer	el **abogado**
teacher	el **maestro**
engineer	el **ingeniero**
nurse	la **enfermera**
accountant	el **contador**

List 89-2

teacher	el **maestro**
lawyer	el **abogado**
nurse	la **enfermera**
engineer	el **ingeniero**
accountant	el **contador**
salesman	el **vendedor**
laborer	el **trabajador**
clerk	el **dependiente**
mechanic	el **mecánico**
merchant	el **comerciante**

List 89-3

laborer	el **trabajador**
salesman	el **vendedor**
mechanic	el **mecánico**
clerk	el **dependiente**
merchant	el **comerciante**
teacher	el **maestro**
nurse	la **enfermera**
lawyer	el **abogado**
accountant	el **contador**
engineer	el **ingeniero**

Self-Test 89

laborer	_____
salesman	_____
mechanic	_____
clerk	_____
merchant	_____
teacher	_____
nurse	_____
lawyer	_____
accountant	_____
engineer	_____

Basic
Básico

List 90-1

college	el **colegio**
answer	la **respuesta**
question	la **pregunta**
student	el **estudiante**
example	el **ejemplo**
life	la **vida**
rich	**rico**
poor	**pobre**
true	**verdadero**
false	**falso**

List 90-2

rich	**rico**
life	la **vida**
true	**verdadero**
poor	**pobre**
false	**falso**
college	el **colegio**
question	la **pregunta**
answer	la **respuesta**
example	el **ejemplo**
student	el **estudiante**

List 90-3

question	la **pregunta**
college	el **colegio**
example	el **ejemplo**
answer	la **respuesta**
student	el **estudiante**
rich	**rico**
true	**verdadero**
life	la **vida**
false	**falso**
poor	**pobre**

Self-Test 90

question	_____
college	_____
example	_____
answer	_____
student	_____
rich	_____
true	_____
life	_____
false	_____
poor	_____

List 91-1

many	muchos
few	pocos
big	grande
small	pequeño
high	alto
low	bajo
word	la palabra
message	el mensaje
idea	la idea
fact	hecho

List 91-2

word	la palabra
low	bajo
idea	la idea
message	el mensaje
fact	hecho
many	muchos
big	grande
few	pocos
high	alto
small	pequeño

List 91-3

big	grande
many	muchos
high	alto
few	pocos
small	pequeño
word	la palabra
idea	la idea
low	bajo
fact	hecho
message	el mensaje

Self-Test 91

big	_____
many	_____
high	_____
few	_____
small	_____
word	_____
idea	_____
low	_____
fact	_____
message	_____

Dialogue 24A

A: What do you do?

B: I'm a student.

A: How is life in college?

B: It's easy.

A: What do you mean?

B: For example, I don't work, I only learn facts and a few ideas.

A: Go on.

B: Then I answer true or false to the teacher's questions.

A: ¿Qué hace usted?

B: Soy estudiante.

A: ¿Cómo va la vida en el colegio?

B: Es fácil.

A: ¿Qué quiere decir?

B: Por ejemplo, no trabajo, aprendo sólo los hechos y unas pocas ideas.

A: Siga.

B: Entonces, contesto verdadero o falso a las preguntas del maestro.

Dialogue 24B

A: Are you the salesman?

B: No, I'm the clerk, the salesman is right there.

A: Thank you. Excuse me, do you sell books on different occupations?

B: Yes, I believe we have some on the professions of law, engineering, and accounting.

A: Do you have a book on nursing?

B: Maybe, I'm going to look. I'm sorry, we don't have any.

A: ¿Es Ud. el vendedor?

B: No, soy el dependiente, el vendedor está allí mismo.

A: Gracias. Perdone, ¿venden ustedes libros sobre ocupaciones diferentes?

B: Creo que sí, tenemos algunos sobre las profesiones de abogado, ingeniero y contador.

A: ¿Tiene un libro sobre enfermería?

B: Quizás, voy a buscar. Lo siento, no lo tenemos.

List 92-1

government	el **gobierno**
God	el **Dios**
nation	la **nación**
people	la **gente**
problem	el **problema**
place	el **lugar**
society	la **sociedad**
street	la **calle**
world	el **mundo**
weather	el **tiempo**

List 92-2

society	la **sociedad**
place	el **lugar**
world	el **mundo**
street	la **calle**
weather	el **tiempo**
government	el **gobierno**
nation	la **nación**
God	el **Dios**
problem	el **problema**
people	la **gente**

List 92-3

nation	la **nación**
government	el **gobierno**
problem	el **problema**
God	el **Dios**
people	la **gente**
society	la **sociedad**
world	el **mundo**
place	el **lugar**
weather	el **tiempo**
street	la **calle**

Self-Test 92

nation	_____
government	_____
problem	_____
God	_____
people	_____
society	_____
world	_____
place	_____
weather	_____
street	_____

List 93-1

if	**aunque (si)**
both	**ambos**
until	**hasta**
while	**mientras**
strong	**fuerte**
each	**cada**
always	**siempre**
never	**nunca**
around	**alrededor de**
memory	la **memoria**

List 93-2

always	**siempre**
each	**cada**
around	**alrededor de**
never	**nunca**
memory	la **memoria**
if	**aunque (si)**
until	**hasta**
both	**ambos**
strong	**fuerte**
while	**mientras**

List 93-3

until	**hasta**
if	**aunque (si)**
strong	**fuerte**
both	**ambos**
while	**mientras**
always	**siempre**
around	**alrededor de**
each	**cada**
memory	la **memoria**
never	**nunca**

Self-Test 93

until	_____
if	_____
strong	_____
both	_____
while	_____
always	_____
around	_____
each	_____
memory	_____
never	_____

Clergy and Government Officials
Los clérigos y los oficiales del gobierno

List 94-1

priest	un sacerdote
minister	un ministro
rabbi	un rabí
nun	una monja
clergyman	un clérigo
mayor	el alcalde
governor	el gobernador
senator	el senador
councilman	el concejal
judge	el juez

List 94-2

governor	el gobernador
mayor	el alcalde
councilman	el concejal
senator	el senador
judge	el juez
priest	un sacerdote
rabbi	un rabí
minister	un ministro
clergyman	un clérigo
nun	una monja

List 94-3

rabbi	un rabí
priest	un sacerdote
clergyman	un clérigo
minister	un ministro
nun	una monja
governor	el gobernador
councilman	el concejal
mayor	el alcalde
judge	el juez
senator	el senador

Self-Test 94

rabbi	_____
priest	_____
clergyman	_____
minister	_____
nun	_____
governor	_____
councilman	_____
mayor	_____
judge	_____
senator	_____

Dialogue 25A

A: Hello!

B: Hello!

A: Where are you from, England?

B: No, from the United States.

A: And you work here?

B: No, I'm on vacation, I work in New York, I'm a representative. And you?

A: I'm also a government official, a representative in Madrid. Let's talk about some government problems.

A: ¡Hola!

B: ¡Hola!

A: ¿De dónde es usted, Inglaterra?

B: No, de los Estados Unidos.

A: ¿Y trabaja aquí?

B: No, estoy de vacaciones, trabajo en Nueva York, soy concejal. ¿Y usted?

A: También soy oficial de gobierno, representante en Madrid. Vamos hablar sobre algunos problemas del gobierno.

Dialogue 25B

A: Do you know Mexico?

B: No, I was never in Mexico, but I visited Spain for a year and I liked it a lot.

A: What did you like the most?

B: I liked most the ambiance of Seville and the hills and mountains around some of the cities. I'll always have good memories of Spain, the nation, and its society.

A: ¿Conoce México?

B: No, nunca estuve en México, pero he visitado España por un año y me gustó mucho.

A: ¿Qué le gustó más?

B: Me gustó el ambiente de Sevilla más y las colinas y montañas alrededor de algunas ciudades. Siempre voy a tener buenos recuerdos de España, la nación y su sociedad.

Measures and Sciences
Las medidas y las ciencias

List 95-1

mile	la **milla**
meter	el **metro**
kilometer	el **kilómetro**
minute	el **minuto**
century	el **siglo**
chemistry	la **química**
physics	la **física**
psychology	la **psicología**
biology	la **biología**
mathematics	las **matemáticas**

List 95-2

physics	la **física**
chemistry	la **química**
biology	la **biología**
psychology	la **psicología**
mathematics	las **matemáticas**
mile	la **milla**
kilometer	el **kilómetro**
meter	el **metro**
century	el **siglo**
minute	el **minuto**

List 95-3

kilometer	el **kilómetro**
mile	la **milla**
century	el **siglo**
meter	el **metro**
minute	el **minuto**
physics	la **física**
biology	la **biología**
chemistry	la **química**
mathematics	las **matemáticas**
psychology	la **psicología**

Self-Test 95

kilometer	_____
mile	_____
century	_____
meter	_____
minute	_____
physics	_____
biology	_____
chemistry	_____
mathematics	_____
psychology	_____

Nature
La naturaleza

List 96-1

mountain	la **montaña**
valley	el **valle**
ocean	el **océano**
hill	la **colina**
river	el **río**
lake	el **lago**
island	la **isla**
stream	el **arroyo**
sea	el/la **mar**
bay	la **bahía**

List 96-2

island	la **isla**
lake	el **lago**
sea	el/la **mar**
stream	el **arroyo**
bay	la **bahía**
mountain	la **montaña**
ocean	el **océano**
valley	el **valle**
river	el **río**
hill	la **colina**

List 96-3

ocean	el **océano**
mountain	la **montaña**
river	el **río**
valley	el **valle**
hill	la **colina**
island	la **isla**
sea	el/la **mar**
lake	el **lago**
bay	la **bahía**
stream	el **arroyo**

Self-Test 96

ocean	_____
mountain	_____
river	_____
valley	_____
hill	_____
island	_____
sea	_____
lake	_____
bay	_____
stream	_____

Flowers and Insects
Las Flores y los insectos

List 97-1

rose	la **rosa**
tulip	el **tulipán**
carnation	el **clavel**
daisy	la **margarita**
grass	la **hierba**
flies	unas **moscas**
ants	unas **hormigas**
bees	unas **abejas**
spider	una **araña**
butterfly	una **mariposa**

List 97-2

ants	unas **hormigas**
flies	unas **moscas**
spider	una **araña**
bees	unas **abejas**
butterfly	una **mariposa**
rose	la **rosa**
carnation	el **clavel**
tulip	el **tulipán**
grass	la **hierba**
daisy	la **margarita**

List 97-3

carnation	el **clavel**
rose	la **rosa**
grass	la **hierba**
tulip	el **tulipán**
daisy	la **margarita**
ants	unas **hormigas**
spider	una **araña**
flies	unas **moscas**
butterfly	una **mariposa**
bees	unas **abejas**

Self-Test 97

carnation	_____
rose	_____
grass	_____
tulip	_____
daisy	_____
ants	_____
spider	_____
flies	_____
butterfly	_____
bees	_____

Dialogue 26A

A: Excuse me, I want to visit the Prado Museum, is this the subway to the Prado Drive?

B: Yes, it's not far, only about two kilometers.

A: Also, please, where is the botanical garden?

B: Near the museum, it's big with miles of flowers— there are roses, tulips, daisies, and many others.

Dialogue 26B

A: Is this the bus from Madrid to Toledo or Avila?

B: Yes, to both.

A: Thank you, are they far?

B: No, about 71 kilometers or 44 miles to Toledo, and 115 kilometers or 71 miles to Avila. You are going to go over the river, up some low hills and then a high mountain. But the trip is slow, you will like it better if you bring something to eat.

A: Thanks a lot.

A: Perdone, quiero visitar al museo del Prado, ¿es éste el metro a Paseo del Prado?

B: Sí, no está lejos, sólo unos dos kilómetros.

A: También, por favor, ¿dónde está el jardín de botánica?

B: Cerca del museo, es grande con millas de flores—hay rosas, tulipanes, margaritas y muchas otras.

A: ¿Es este el autobús de Madrid a Toledo o Ávila?

B: Sí, ambos.

A: Gracias, ¿están lejos?

B: No, más o menos setenta y un kilómetros o cuarenta y cuatro millas a Toledo, y ciento quince kilómetros o setenta y un millas a Ávila. Va a ir sobre el río, arriba de algunas colinas bajas, y después una montaña alta. Pero el viaje es lento, le va a gustar más si trae algo para comer.

A: Muchas gracias.

Animals
Animales

List 98-1

dog	el **perro**
cat	el **gato**
horse	el **caballo**
cow	la **vaca**
lion	el **león**
tiger	el **tigre**
elephant	el **elefante**
pig	el **puerco**
bear	el **oso**
mouse	el **ratón**

List 98-2

elephant	el **elefante**
tiger	el **tigre**
bear	el **oso**
pig	el **puerco**
mouse	el **ratón**
dog	el **perro**
horse	el **caballo**
cat	el **gato**
lion	el **león**
cow	la **vaca**

List 98-3

horse	el **caballo**
dog	el **perro**
lion	el **león**
cat	el **gato**
cow	la **vaca**
elephant	el **elefante**
bear	el **oso**
tiger	el **tigre**
mouse	el **ratón**
pig	el **puerco**

Self-Test 98

horse	_____
dog	_____
lion	_____
cat	_____
cow	_____
elephant	_____
bear	_____
tiger	_____
mouse	_____
pig	_____

Birds
Los pájaros

List 99-1

robin	el petirrojo
sparrow	el gorrión
cardinal	el cardenal
eagle	el águila
crow	el cuervo
canary	el canario
parakeet	el perico
owl	la lechuza
dove	la paloma
parrot	la cotorra

List 99-2

parakeet	el perico
canary	el canario
dove	la paloma
owl	la lechuza
parrot	la cotorra
robin	el petirrojo
cardinal	el cardenal
sparrow	el gorrión
crow	el cuervo
eagle	el águila

List 99-3

cardinal	el cardenal
robin	el petirrojo
crow	el cuervo
sparrow	el gorrión
eagle	el águila
parakeet	el perico
dove	la paloma
canary	el canario
parrot	la cotorra
owl	la lechuza

Self-Test 99

cardinal	_____
robin	_____
crow	_____
sparrow	_____
eagle	_____
parakeet	_____
dove	_____
canary	_____
parrot	_____
owl	_____

Countries
Los países

List 100-1

France	**Francia**
United States	**Estados Unidos**
Russia	**Rusia**
England	**Inglaterra**
Germany	**Alemania**
Canada	**Canadá**
Italy	**Italia**
Spain	**España**
Mexico	**México**
China	**China**
Japan	**Japón**

List 100-2

Canada	**Canadá**
Germany	**Alemania**
England	**Inglaterra**
Mexico	**México**
Spain	**España**
Japan	**Japón**
Russia	**Rusia**
Italy	**Italia**
United States	**Estados Unidos**
France	**Francia**
China	**China**

List 100-3

Mexico	**México**
Italy	**Italia**
Japan	**Japón**
Canada	**Canadá**
United States	**Estados Unidos**
England	**Inglaterra**
China	**China**
Russia	**Rusia**
France	**Francia**
Germany	**Alemania**
Spain	**España**

Self-Test 100

Mexico	_____
Italy	_____
Japan	_____
Canada	_____
United States	_____
England	_____
China	_____
Russia	_____
France	_____
Germany	_____
Spain	_____

Dialogue 27A

A: Yesterday, Sunday afternoon, I saw a soccer game, now I want to visit the zoo.

B: Why?

A: Because I always enjoy going in a boat on the lake and seeing the birds.

B: Very well, let's see some canaries, robins, and crows—but I don't want to see the animals.

A: Ayer, domingo en la tarde, vi un partido de balompié, ahora quiero visitar al zoológico.

B: ¿Por qué?

A: Porque siempre me gusta ir en una bote en el lago y ver los pájaros.

B: Muy bien, vamos a ver unos canarios, petirrojos y cuervos—pero no quiero ver los animales.

Dialogue 27B

A: Do you want to visit Spain again?

B: Yes, there are other places I want to see. On our next vacation let's see the southern cities—Cadiz by the Atlantic ocean and Malaga by the Mediterranean sea, both are in Andalusia. And after that we can visit Italy or Germany.

A: Okay, but after Spain I prefer to visit France.

A: ¿Quiere visitar España otra vez?

B: Sí, hay otros lugares que quiero ver. En nuestras próximas vacaciones vamos a ver las ciudades del sur—Cádiz por el océano Atlántico y Málaga por el mar Mediterráneo, ambos están en Andalucía. Y después de eso podemos visitar a Italia o Alemania.

A: Bueno, pero después de España prefiero visitar a Francia.

Review Test 3

List	Test Words	Answer
67	juice	_____
	wine	_____
68	fried	_____
	dessert	_____
69	raw	_____
	baked	_____
70	pineapple	_____
	bowl	_____
71	onion	_____
	squash	_____
72	to find	_____
	thirst	_____
73	to read	_____
	which?	_____
74	magazine	_____
	sports	_____
75	song	_____
	drum	_____
76	I bought	_____
	we ate	_____
77	you could	_____
	she wanted	_____
78	we went	_____
	I gave	_____
79	you came	_____
	I saw	_____

List	Test Words	Answer (continued)
80	expensive	*Caro*
	walk	*andar*
81	corduroy	
	scarf	*Bufan*
82	ring	*anill*
	necklace	
83	skin	*piel*
	hair	*pelo*
84	chest	*pecho*
	fingernail	*uña*
85	blister	
	fever	
86	clean	*limpu*
	old	*rey*
87	thing	*cosa*
	because	
88	to work	*Trataja*
	to sell	*vendu*
89	lawyer	*abogado*
	nurse	*enfermer*
90	example	*ejemplo*
	answer	*respuesta*
91	word	*palabra*
	fact	*hecho*
92	world	*mundo*
	place	*lugar*
93	until	*hasta*
	always	*siempre*

List	Test Words	Answer *(continued)*
94	judge	
	priest	
95	mile	
	century	
96	bay	
	valley	
97	daisy	
	butterfly	
98	bear	
	cat	
99	dove	
	eagle	
100	France	
	Japan	

Useful Expressions

Greetings

Good morning.	**Buenos días.**
Good afternoon.	**Buenas tardes.**
Good evening./Good night.	**Buenas noches.**
Yes/No	**Sí/No**
How do you do?	**¿Cómo le va? (¿Cómo está Ud.?)**
I am fine, thank you.	**Estoy bien, gracias.**
I am pleased to meet you.	**Mucho gusto en conocerle.**
Do you speak English?	**¿Habla inglés?**
I don't speak much Spanish.	**Yo no hablo mucho español.**
Please repeat.	**Repita, por favor.**
How do you say . . . ?	**¿Cómo se dice...?**
Speak slowly, please.	**Hable despacio, por favor.**
Thank you very much.	**Muchas gracias.**
You're welcome.	**De nada.**
Excuse me.	**Con permiso.**
Please help me.	**Ayúdeme, por favor.**
Can you translate this?	**¿Me lo puede traducir?**
Do you understand?	**¿Comprende?**
I understand.	**Comprendo.**
I don't understand.	**No comprendo.**
I'm lost.	**Estoy perdido (perdida).**

Do you have a map?	¿Tiene un mapa?
Where are the toilets?	¿Dónde están los servicios?
Please, show me.	Enséñeme, por favor.
Please point.	Indique, por favor.
Good luck.	¡Buena suerte!
Good-bye.	¡Adiós!
See you later.	Hasta luego.

Telling Time

What time is it?	*¿Qué hora es?*
It's early.	Es temprano.
It's (too) late.	Ya es (muy) tarde.
It's noon.	Es mediodía.
It's midnight.	Es medianoche.
In the morning	*Por la mañana*
It's one o'clock (a.m.).	Es la una (de la mañana).
It's five o'clock (a.m.).	Son las cinco (de la mañana).
In the afternoon or evening	*Por la tarde o por la noche*
It's three o'clock (p.m.).	Son las tres (de la tarde).
It's four o'clock (p.m.).	Son las cuatro (de la tarde).
It's seven o'clock (p.m.).	Son las siete (de la noche).
Past the hour	*Después de la hora*
It's ten past six.	Son las seis y diez.
It's a quarter past seven.	Son las siete y cuarto.
It's twenty past eight.	Son las ocho y veinte.
It's half past nine.	Son las nueve y media.
Before the hour	*Antes de la hora*
It's twenty to ten.	Son las diez menos veinte.
It's a quarter to eleven.	Son las once menos cuarto.

It's five to five.	Son las cinco menos cinco.
At what time (does the train leave)?	*¿A qué hora (sale el tren)?*
At 18:00 (6 p.m.).	A las dieciocho.
At 20:00 (8 p.m.).	A las veinte.
At 21:30 (9:30 p.m.).	A las veintiuna y media.
In fifteen minutes.	En quince minutos.
In half an hour.	En media hora.

At the Table

I am hungry.	Tengo hambre.
We want breakfast.	Queremos desayunar.
Where is there a restaurant?	¿Dónde hay un restaurante?
Are you thirsty?	¿Tiene sed?
What would you like to drink?	¿Qué quiere beber?
Would you like some coffee?	¿Quiere café?
This is delicious.	Esto es delicioso.
Thank you for making my lunch.	Gracias por hacer mi comida.
What's on the menu?	¿Que tiene el menú?
I'm a vegetarian.	Soy vegetariano (vegetariana).
Just a small portion.	Sólo una porción pequeña.
Thank you, could I have a little more?	Gracias, ¿podría tener un poco más?
May I help myself to a cup of coffee?	¿Puedo servirme una taza de café?
I'd like a dessert, please.	Quiero un postre, por favor.
Nothing more, thanks.	Nada más, gracias.
The dinner was very good.	La cena estuvo muy buena.
Thanks for your hospitality.	Gracias por su hospitalidad.

Telephone

May I use your telephone?	¿Puedo usar su teléfono?
May I make a long distance call?	¿Puedo hacer una llamada de larga distancia?
I want to call . . .	Quiero llamar...
Can I dial direct?	¿Puedo marcar directo?
How do I get the operator?	¿Cómo obtengo la operadora?
I want to place a credit card call.	Quiero hacer una llamada por cobrar.
Extension . . . please.	Extensión... por favor.
We were cut off.	Nos hemos cortado.
Would you please take a message?	¿Puede tomar un mensaje, por favor?
Just a moment, please.	Un momento, por favor.
Call me when you are ready to go.	Llámame cuando esté listo (lista).

Mail

Did the mail come today?	¿Hay correo hoy?
Where can I mail these letters?	¿Dónde puedo echar estas cartas?
I'd like a stamp for this letter to the United States.	Quiero una estampilla para mandar esta carta a Estados Unidos.
What's the postage for a postcard to Canada?	¿Cuánto es el precio para una tarjeta para Canadá?

Shopping

May I help you?	¿Cómo puedo servirle?
No thanks.	No gracias.

I'm just looking.	Estoy mirando nada más.
Help me, please.	Ayúdeme, por favor.
I'm looking for . . .	Estoy buscando...
I want to buy . . .	Quiero comprar...
Bring me . . .	Tráigame...
Show me what you have.	Muéstreme lo que tiene.
How much does this cost?	¿Cuánto es?
It is too much.	Es demasiado.
What size do you think I need?	¿Qué talla cree que necesito?
May I try this on?	¿Puedo probármelo?
Where is the dressing room?	¿Dónde está el cuarto de vestir?
Can you order it for me?	¿Puede ordenármelo?
I'll take it with me.	Me lo llevo.
I would like to cash a check.	Quiero cambiar un cheque.
Do you have identification?	¿Tiene cartilla?
I'd like to return this.	Quiero cambiar esto.
Here's the receipt.	Aquí tiene su recibo.

A Short Guide to Spanish Grammar

Subject Pronouns

The following are the subject pronouns:

Singular		*Plural*	
I	yo	*we*	nosotros
you	tú		
he	él	*they*	ellos (male, or male and female)
she	ella		ellas (female only)
you	usted	*you*	ustedes (plural)

In this book, we give the forms used in formal or polite speech for *you* (**usted, ustedes**). We do not generally provide those used in familiar speech (**tú**). *You* is often abbreviated as: **Ud.** or **Uds.**

In Spanish, subject pronouns are generally not said or written, since they are understood by the differences in endings of verb forms. However, they are sometimes used for clarification. For example, **¿Tiene Ud. los billetes?** (*Do you have the tickets?*)

Present Tense of Verbs

The basic infinitive form of verbs ends in **-ar, -er,** or **-ir**: for example, **hablar** (*to speak*), **comprender** (*to understand*), and **escribir** (*to write*). Those endings are dropped and replaced for different subject pronouns as follows:

For **-ar** verbs:

I	-o	hablo
you/he/she	-a	habla
we	-amos	hablamos
(plural) *you/they*	-an	hablan

For -**er** verbs:

I	-o	comprendo
you/he/she	-e	comprende
we	-emos	comprendemos
(plural) *you/they*	-en	comprenden

For -**ir** verbs:

I	-o	escribo
you/he/she	-e	escribe
we	-imos	escribimos
(plural) *you/they*	-iben	escriben

Remember that the same verb form is used for *you*, *he*, *she*, or *it* in the singular. *They* or *you* in the plural also share the same form. (Note that end glossaries to this book give verb forms for *I*, *you* (formal singular), *we*, and *they*.)

Some verbs have irregular forms, such as **pensar** (*to think*), **yo pienso.** The end glossaries give them in their unique forms.

The Verbs "to Be" in Spanish

Ser and **estar** both mean *to be*, but each verb has different uses. Both verbs are irregular. **Ser** is used:

- with predicate nouns and pronouns, e.g., **Miguel es doctor.** (*Michael is a doctor.*) **Soy yo.** (*It is I.*)
- with adjectives for characteristic or permanent qualities, e.g., **Él es mi sobrino.** (*He is my nephew.*)

- for origin, ownership, or material (followed by **de**), e.g., **El traje es de lana.** (*The suit is wool.*)
- for impersonal expressions and the time of day, e.g., **Es tarde.** (*It is late.*)

Estar is used:

- for location, e.g., **¿Dónde está la biblioteca?** (*Where is the library?*)
- with temporary conditions and health, e.g., **Estoy mareado.** (*I am dizzy.*), **¿Cómo está Ud.?** (*How are you?*)

Note: The past tense forms of **ser** are the same as those for **ir** (*to go*), e.g., **fui** (*I was* or *I went*). The context gives the meaning: **Fui soltero hasta ayer.** (*I was single until yesterday.*) **Fui al hotel después de cena.** (*I went to the hotel after dinner.*)

The Verbs "to Know" in Spanish

Saber and **conocer** both mean *to know*, but each verb has a different use and both are irregular.

Use **saber** to talk about knowing facts, languages, or how to do something, e.g., **Lo sé.** (*I know it.*), **¿Sabe Ud. inglés?** (*Do you know English?*), **No sé nadar.** (*I don't know how to swim.*)

Use **conocer** to talk about familiarity with people and places, e.g., **¿Conoce Ud. a Juan?** (*Do you know John?*), and **Conozco Madrid.** (*I know/am acquainted with Madrid.*)

The Verb Gustar

Gustar is used to express likes and dislikes. Only two forms are used, third person plural and third person singular: **Gusta** is used when the thing liked is singular. **Gustan** is used when the thing liked is plural. Compare:

I like the city.	**Me <u>gusta</u> la ciudad.**
I like the stores.	**Me <u>gustan</u> las tiendas.**

The appropriate pronoun (indirect object pronoun) **me** (for *I*), **le** (for *he/she/it/you*), **nos** (for *we*), or **les** (for *they/you* plural) is inserted to express who likes.

Do you like the suit?	¿**Le** gusta el traje?
Yes, I like it.	Sí, **me** gusta.
Do you (pl.) like the museum?	¿**Les** gusta el museo?
Yes, we like it.	Sí, **nos** gusta.
Do you like my relatives?	¿**Le** gustan mis parientes?
Yes, I like them.	Sí, **me** gustan.

To answer "no," you say:

No, I don't like them.	**No, no me gustan.**
Do you like the restaurant?	¿**Le** gusta el restaurante?
No, I don't like the restaurant.	**No, no me gusta.**

Reflexive Verbs

A reflexive verb is one whose subject acts upon itself, e.g., *He washes himself*—**Él se lava.** Many verbs are reflexive in Spanish but not in English, e.g., *to get up*—**levantarse.**

Some verbs, not usually reflexive, can become reflexive and change in meaning; for example: *to do*—**hacer,** *to become*—**hacerse,** and *to put*—**poner,** *to put on*—**ponerse.**

The reflexive verbs are conjugated like other verbs; however, each verb form is accompanied by a reflexive pronoun of the same number and person as the subject.

The reflexive pronouns are as follows:

myself	**me**
yourself (familiar)	**te**
himself, herself, yourself, itself	**se**
ourselves	**nos**
themselves, yourselves	**se**

In reflexive verbs, the reflexive pronoun generally precedes the conjugated verb form. For example, *to go to bed*—**acostarse.**

I go to bed	**me acuesto**
you (fam.) *go to bed*	**te acuestas**
he/she goes to bed, you go to bed	**se acuesta**
we go to bed	**nos acostamos**
you/they go to bed	**se acuestan**

The reflexive pronoun follows and is attached to the verb in the infinitive, e.g. *He's going to get up at 6 (a.m.)*—**Va a levantarse a las seis (de la mañana)**. The reflexive pronoun **se** is also used in a general or impersonal way to mean *one, they,* or *you.* For example:

You go out this way.	**Se sale por aquí.**
They say smoking is forbidden.	**Se dice se prohibe fumar.**
One (They) washes one's (their) hands.	**Se lavan los manos.**

Past Tense of Verbs

The past (preterit) tense of verbs is formed by dropping the infinitive endings -**ar**, -**er**, -**ir**, and adding the following endings:

For -**ar** verbs:

I	-**é**	**hablé**
you/he/she	-**ó**	**habló**
we	-**amos**	**hablamos**
(plural) *you/they*	-**aron**	**hablaron**

For -**er** and -**ir** verbs:

I	-**í**	**comprendí**
you/he/she	-**ió**	**comprendió**
we	-**imos**	**complendimos**
(plural) *you/they*	-**ieron**	**complendieron**

Verbs with irregular forms, such as **poder** (*to be able*), **tener** (*to have*), **querer** (*to want*), **ir** (*to go*), and **estar** (*to be*), must be learned separately.

The Future Tense

The future tense is formed by adding the following endings to the entire verb infinitive (of all verbs, **-ar, -er,** and **-ir**):

I	-é	escribiré
you/he/she	-á	escribirá
we	-emos	escribiremos
(plural) *you/they*	-án	escribirán

For example, **compraré** (*I shall buy*), **comeré** (*I shall eat*), and **viviré** (*I shall live*). (Note that future tense forms are not given in the word lists at the end of this book.)

To express the future informally, it is easier for the beginner to use the present tense of **ir** (*to go*), adding **a** plus the infinitive of the appropriate verb, e.g., **Voy a comer.** (*I am going to eat.*) **Mis amigos van a venir en coche.** (*My friends are going to come by car.*)

Infinitive of Verbs

The infinitive of most verbs is reformed by adding the letter **-r** to the *you* form of the verb. Examine the following sentences:

You take a taxi to the airport.	**Toma un taxi al aeropuerto.**
You are going <u>to take</u> a taxi to the airport.	**Va a <u>tomar</u> un taxi al aeropuerto.**
You buy gifts for your family.	**Compra regalos para su familia.**
You are going <u>to buy</u> gifts for your family.	**Va a <u>comprar</u> regalos para su familia.**

When two verbs follow each other in Spanish, the second one is always in the infinitive, e.g., **Voy a <u>ir</u> al aeropuerto.** (*I am going to go to the airport.*) **Pienso <u>salir</u>.** (*I think I'll leave.*)

Direct and Indirect Object Pronouns

The direct object pronouns are **me** (*me*), **te** (*you*), **lo, la** (*him/her/it*), **nos** (*us*), **las, los** (*them*).

Use **lo(s)** and **la(s)** when referring to masculine and feminine objects and people. For example, **¿Conoce a mis hermanos?** (*Do you know my brothers?*) **Sí, los conozco.** (*Yes, I know them.*) **¿Tiene la dirección?** (*Do you have the address?*) **Lo siento, no la tengo.** (*I'm sorry, I don't have it.*) (Note: In some parts of Spain, when referring to males and masculine nouns, the direct object **le[s]** is used instead of **lo[s]**.)

Some verbs take an indirect instead of a direct object, e.g., *He speaks to me* (not *He speaks me*).

The only difference in the forms of the direct and indirect objects is in the third-person singular and plural (*he/she/you/it*) and (*them/you*). Use **le** for the singular (*to him/to her/ to you/to it*) and **les** for the plural (*to the/to you*); for example, **Le habla.** (*He speaks to him/her/you.*) **Les habla.** (*He speaks to them/you.*)

To avoid ambiguity, you may add **a él, a ella, a Ud., a ellos, a ellas, a Uds**; for example, **Le doy el libro a ella.** (*I gave the book to her.*)

Descriptive Adjectives

Adjectives must agree in number and gender (masculine/feminine) of the noun described. They are usually placed after the noun. For example:

a rich uncle	**un tío rico**	*rich uncles*	**tíos ricos**
a rich aunt	**una tía rica**	*rich aunts*	**tías ricas**

Adjectives ending in -e or in a consonant do not change in the feminine. The plural form for both genders ends in -**es.** For example:

a strong man	**un hombre fuerte**	*strong men*	**hombres fuertes**
a strong glue	**una cola fuerte**	*strong glues*	**colas fuertes**

Possessive Adjectives

my book	**mi libro**	*our relative*	**nuestro pariente**
my books	**mis libros**	*our relatives*	**nuestros parientes**

your dress	**su vestido**	*our suitcase*	**nuestra maleta**
your dresses	**sus vestidos**	*our suitcases*	**nuestras maletas**

Su is used for *his, her, its, your,* or *their* and precedes the object or person "owned." **Sus** is the plural form. The context usually indicates who or what the possessor is, but you may clarify with an appropriate pronoun, as:

	su amigo
his friend	**el amigo de él**
her friend	**el amigo de ella**
your friend	**el amigo de Ud.**
their friend	**el amigo de ellos**

Demonstrative Adjectives

The demonstrative adjective *this* is **este** in the masculine form and **esta** in the feminine. The corresponding plurals are **estos** and **estas**. *That* is **ese/esa** and *those* is **esos/esas**.

this finger	**este dedo**	*that ring*	**ese anillo**
this hand	**esta mano**	*that scarf*	**esa bufanda**

Adverbs

The adverb is usually formed from the feminine form of an adjective (if the adjective has a feminine form) by adding **-mente**.

I only eat vegetables.	**Yo como solamente legumbres.**
They walk slowly.	**Caminaron lentamente.**

Be careful not to confuse the adverbs **bien** and **mal** (which generally modify verbs) with the adjectives **bueno** and **malo** (which modify nouns).

She speaks English well.	**Ella habla bien inglés.**
She speaks very good English.	**Ella habla un inglés muy bueno.**

Prepositions

Prepositions make a connection between nouns or pronouns and other parts of speech. For example:

She is at this hotel.	**Ella está <u>en</u> este hotel.**
I came home from the hospital.	**Llegué a casa <u>del</u> hospital.**
We walked to the park after dinner.	**Andamos <u>al</u> parque <u>después de</u> la cena.**

The use of prepositions can only be learned by observation. Pay close attention to their relationship with the words with which they are usually found.

Some of the most commonly used prepositions are:

at   *at,* at a location (<u>en</u> **de localidad**), e.g., *at school*—**<u>en</u> la escuela,** *at work*—**<u>en</u> el trabajo**
at, toward (<u>a</u>, **hacia**), e.g., *look <u>at</u>*—**mirar <u>a</u>,** *arrive <u>at</u>*—**llegar <u>a</u>**
at, for the time (<u>a</u>, **para el tiempo**), e.g., *<u>at</u> noon*—**<u>al</u> mediodía,** *<u>at</u> night*—**<u>por</u> la noche**

by   *by,* for nearness (<u>por</u> **de proximidad**), e.g., *<u>by</u> the platform*—**<u>por</u> el andén**
by, by means of (<u>por</u>, **mediante**), e.g., *<u>by</u> train*—**<u>por</u> el tren**
by, in by tonight (<u>para</u>, **en <u>para esta noche</u>**), e.g., *The lesson will be finished <u>by</u> Tuesday*—**La lección estará terminado <u>para</u> el martes.**

for   **<u>para</u>**—e.g., *That one is <u>for</u> him*—**Esa es <u>para</u> él,** *<u>for</u> dancing*—**<u>para</u> bailar**
<u>por</u>—e.g., *<u>for</u> a minute*—**<u>por</u> un minuto,** *<u>for</u> a long time*—**<u>por</u> mucho tiempo**
for or *as* (<u>de</u> o **<u>como</u>**), e.g., *I ate eggs <u>for</u> lunch*—**Comí huevos <u>de</u> comida,** *He used a knife <u>as</u> a can opener*—**Él usó un cuchillo <u>como</u> abrelatas.**

from   *from* or *preceding* (<u>de</u> o <u>desde</u> de precedente), e.g., *from Spain to Canada*—<u>de</u> España a Canadá, *from two to four in the afternoon*—<u>de</u> las dos a las cuarto en el tarde

in   *in* or *inside* (<u>en</u> o <u>adentro</u>), e.g., *in two hours*—<u>en</u> dos horas, *in the car*—<u>en</u> el coche

of   <u>de</u>, e.g., *made of wool*—hecho <u>de</u> lana, *the city of New York*—la ciudad <u>de</u> Nueva York

to   *to* as in direction (<u>a</u> de dirección), e.g., *to the theatre*—<u>al</u> teatro, *to Italy*—<u>a</u> Italia

with   <u>con</u>, meaning *union* or *together with* (significado de unión), e.g., *with her*—<u>con</u> ella, *I ate it with some sugar*—Lo comí <u>con</u> un poco de azúcar

Some other prepositions:

before	antes de	*after*	después de
down	abajo	*during*	durante
around	alrededor de	*until*	hasta
up	arriba	*without*	sin

Resources

Dictionaries

Harper Collins Spanish-English, English-Spanish Dictionary.
    México D.F., México: Editorial Grijalbo, 1992.
Larousse Diccionario Compacto Español-Inglés, Inglés-Español.
    París: Larousse-Bordas, 1999.
Vox Compact Spanish and English Dictionary, 2nd ed. New York:
    McGraw-Hill, 1994.
Vox Spanish and English School Dictionary. New York: McGraw-
    Hill, 1996.

Internet Pages

Remember that URLs for Internet websites are subject to change. If
a link is no longer available, use a search engine to find your material.

http://globegate.utm.edu/spanish/spandico.html/
Links for general and specialized dictionaries, e.g., golf, math,
    medical terms, political science, wine, etc.

http://www.spainview.com/abbrev.html
Commonly used Spanish abbreviations and acronyms, proverbs,
    false cognates, and over 150 select links on Spain.

http://members.tripod.com/~jdmoncada/spanish.html
General resources with links for grammar, vocabulary, language
    lessons, online dictionaries, translators, newspapers. etc.

http://www.sgci.mec.es/usa/enlaces/
Eighteen categorized links in Spanish or English from the Office of
Education, Spanish Embassy, Washington, DC, covers professional organizations, internet chat rooms, penpals/keypals,
videos/software, etc.

http://www.ushcc.com/
The United States Hispanic Chamber of Commerce identifies busi-
ness opportunities for Hispanic-owned businesses. The website
search engine locates Hispanic suppliers and services.

English-Spanish Glossary

a (feminine)	**una**
a (masculine)	**un**
abdomen	el **abdomen**
abroad	al **extranjero**
accountant	el **contador**
address	la **dirección**
adults	los **mayores**
after	**después de**
afternoon	la **tarde**
again	**otra vez**
airplane	el **avión**
airport	el **aeropuerto**
allergic	**alérgico**
also	**también**
always	**siempre**
am, I	**soy**
am, I	**estoy**
and	**y**
animals	los **animales**
ankle	el **tobillo**
answer	la **respuesta**
answer, to	**contestar**

ants	unas **hormigas**
apartment	un **apartamento**
appetizers	las **tapas**
apples	unas **manzanas**
appointment	la **cita**
April	**abril**
are, they	**están**
are, they	**son**
are, we	**somos**
are, we	**estamos**
are, you	**está**
arm	el **brazo**
around	**alrededor** de
arrival	la **llegada**
arrive, to	**llegar**
article	el **artículo**
as	**como**
ashtray	un **cenicero**
ask, to	**preguntar**
asparagus	el **espárrago**
aspirin	las **aspirinas**
at	**en**
ate, I	**comí**
ate, they	**comieron**
ate, we	**comimos**
ate, you	**comió**
atmosphere	el **ambiente**
August	**agosto**
aunt	la **tía**
autumn	el **otoño**

back	la **espalda**
bacon	el **tocino**
bad	**malo**
bag	un **bolso**
baked	**horneado**
bakery	la **panadería**
bananas	unos **plátanos**
bandage	una **venda**
bank	un **banco**
barbecued	**a la barbacoa**
barber	un **barbero**
barbershop	la **peluquería**
basement	el **sótano**
bathrobe	la **bata**
bathroom	el **baño**
battery	la **batería**
bay	la **bahía**
be, to	**ser**
be able, to	**poder**
be careful, to	**tener cuidado**
be, to	**estar**
beach	la **playa**
beans (kidney)	las **judías**
bear	el **oso**
because	**porque**
bed	la **cama**
bedroom	una **alcoba**
beef	el **buey**
beer	una **cerveza**
bees	unas **abejas**

beets	las **remolachas**
before	**antes**
believe, to	**creer**
belt	un **cinturón**
better	**mejor**
bicycle	la **bicicleta**
big	**grande**
bill	la **cuenta**
biology	la **biología**
birds	los **pájaros**
black	**negro**
black coffee	un **café solo**
blanket	una **manta**
~~blister~~	una **ampolla**
blood	la **sangre**
blouse	una **blusa**
blue	**azul**
boat	el **barco**
boat	el **bote**
boiled	**hervido**
bone	el **hueso**
book	el **libro**
bookstore	la **librería**
boots	las **botas**
botanical	**botánico**
both	**ambos**
bottle	una **botella**
bought, I	**compré**
bought, they	**compraron**
bought, we	**compramos**
bought, you	**compró**

bourbon	un **borbón**
bowl	el **cuenco**
boyfriend	el **novio**
bra	un **sujetador**
bracelet	la **pulsera**
brakes	los **frenos**
brandy	un **coñac**
bras	los **sostenes**
bread	el **pan**
breakfast	el **desayuno**
bring, I	**traigo**
bring, they	**traen**
bring, to	**traer**
bring, we	**traemos**
bring, you	**trae**
broiled	**a la parrilla**
brooch	el **broche**
broom	una **escoba**
brother	el **hermano**
brown	**moreno**
bullfight	la **corrida de toros**
burn	una **quemadura**
bus	el **autobús**
business	el **negocio**
bust	el **busto**
but	**pero**
butcher	la **carnicería**
butter	la **mantequilla**
butterfly	una **mariposa**
buy, to	**comprar**
by	**por**

cabbage	el **repollo**
café	una **cafetería**
cake	la **torta**
call	una **llamada**
call, to	**llamar**
came, I	**vine**
came, they	**vinieron**
came, we	**vinimos**
came, ~~you~~ He	**vino**
camera	una **cámara**
can, I	**puedo**
can opener	un **abrelatas**
can, they	**pueden**
can, we	**podemos**
can, you	**puede**
Canada	**Canadá**
canary	el **canario**
cancer	el **cáncer**
cap	el **gorro**
car	el **coche**
cardinal	el **cardenal**
care	el **cuidado**
careful	**cuidado**
carnation	el **clavel**
carpets	las **alfombras**
carrots	las **zanahorias**
cash, to	**cobrar**
cat	el **gato**
cauliflower	la **coliflor**
caution	la **precaución**
celery	el **apio**

century	el **siglo**
chair	una **silla**
champagne	una **champaña**
change, to	**cambiar**
cheaper	**más barato**
check	el **cheque**
check-out	la **caja**
cheese	el **queso**
chemistry	la **química**
cherries	unas **cerezas**
chest	el **pecho**
chewing gum	un **chicle**
chicken	un **pollo**
children	los **niños**
China	**China**
chocolate	el **chocolate**
chops	unas **chuletas**
church	una **iglesia**
cider	una **sidra**
cigarette	un **cigarrillo**
cinnamon	la **canela**
cities	las **ciudades**
clams	unas **almejas**
clarinet	un **clarinete**
classical	**clásico**
clean	**limpio**
clear	**despejado**
clergyman	un **clérigo**
clerk	el **dependiente**
closed	**cerrado**
closet	un **ropero**

cloudy	**nublado**
coat	el **abrigo**
cod	un **bacalao**
coffee	un **café**
cold (illness)	el **catarro**
cold (adjective)	**frío**
cold cuts	los **fiambres**
collar	el **cuello**
college	el **colegio**
come, I	**vengo**
come in	**adelante**
come, they	**vienen**
come, to	**venir**
come, we	**venimos**
come, you	**viene**
company	una **compañía**
complaints	las **reclamaciones**
concert	el **concierto**
condiments	los **condimentos**
cone (ice cream)	un **barquillo**
constipation	el **estreñimiento**
continue, to	**seguir**
continuous	**continuo**
cookies	las **galletas**
corduroy	la **pana**
corn	el **maíz**
cosmetics	los **cosméticos**
cost	el **coste**
cot	un **catre**
cottage	una **caseta**
cotton	el **algodón**

couch	un sofá
cough	la tos
could, I	pude
could, they	pudieron
could, we	pudimos
could, ~~you~~ *He*	pudo
councilman	el concejal
cousin	el primo
cow	la vaca
crab	un cangrejo
crockery	la vajilla
crossroads	el cruce
crow	el cuervo
cucumber	el pepino
custard	las natillas
daisy	la margarita
dance, to	bailar
danger	el peligro
date	la fecha
daughter	una hija
day	el día
December	diciembre
delicatessen	la mantequería
delighted, to be	encantar
denim	el dril
dentist	un dentista
dentures	la dentadura
deodorant	un desodorante
depart, to	salir
department	la sección

department store	un **almacén**
departure	la **salida**
deposit	la **finanza**
dessert	un **postre**
detour	el **desvío**
diamond	un **diamante**
diarrhea	la **diarrea**
diet	una **dieta**
different	**diferente**
dining room	el **comedor**
dinner	la **cena**
dirty	**sucio**
dizzy	**mareado**
doctor	un **doctor**
dog	el **perro**
dollars	los **dólares**
door	la **puerta**
double	**doble**
dove	la **paloma**
down	**abajo**
drapery	la **pañería**
dream	el **sueño**
dream, to	**soñar**
dress	un **vestido**
dresser	una **cómoda**
drink	una **bebida**
drive	el **paseo**
drugstore	la **droguería**
drum	un **tambor**
dry	**seco**
dry cleaner	una **tintorería**

dry goods	la **lencería**
dull	**sordo**
during	**durante**
dusty	**polvoriento**
each	**cada**
eagle	el **águila (f.)**
ear	la **oreja**
earrings	unos **aretes**
east	el **este**
easy	**fácil**
eat, to	**comer**
eat, I	**como**
eat, they	**comen**
eat, we	**comemos**
eat, you	**come**
egg	un **huevo**
elbow	el **codo**
electricity	la **electricidad**
elephant	el **elefante**
elevator	el **ascensor**
emerald	una **esmeralda**
engineer	el **ingeniero**
England	**Inglaterra**
English	el **inglés**
enough	**basta**
enter, to	**entrar**
entrance	la **entrada**
envelopes	los **sobres**
equipment	el **equipo**
estimate, to	**estimar**

everything	**todo**
example	el **ejemplo**
excuse me	**perdone**
exit	la **salida**
expensive	**caro**
eye	el **ojo**
face	la **cara**
fact	el **hecho**
false	**falso**
family	la **familia**
far	**lejos**
farmhouse	una **alquería**
fast	**rápido**
fat	la **grasa**
father	el **padre**
favorite	**favorito**
February	**febrero**
feel, to	**sentir**
fell, I	**caí**
fever	una **calentura**
feverish	con **fiebre**
few	**pocos**
filling (tooth)	un **empaste**
film	la **película**
find, to	**hallar**
finger	el **dedo**
fingernail	la **uña**
first	**primero**
first name	el **nombre**
fish	el **pescado**

fish market	la **pescadería**
fishing	la **pesca**
flannel	la **franela**
flies (insects)	unas **moscas**
floor	la **planta**; el **piso**
flowers	las **flores**
flu	la **gripe**
follow, to	**seguir**
food	la **alimentación**
foot	el **pie**
for	**para**
fork	un **tenedor**
France	**Francia**
fresh	**fresco**
Friday	el **viernes**
fried	**frito**
friend	un **amigo**
from	**desde**; **de**
frozen foods	los **congelados**
fruit	la **fruta**
frying pan	una **sartén**
full	**lleno**
furniture	los **muebles**
garbage	la **basura**
garden	el **jardín**
garlic	el **ajo**
gas station	la **gasolinera**
gave, I	**di**
Germany	**Alemania**
get, to	**obtener**

get up, to	levantarse
gift	un regalo
gin	una ginebra
give, I	doy
give, to	dar
glass	un vaso
gloves	unos guantes
go, I	voy
go, they	van
go, to	ir
go, we	vamos
go, you	va
God	el Dios
gold	el oro
good	bueno
government	el gobierno
governor	el gobernador
grandfather	el abuelo
grandmother	la abuela
grapefruit	un pomelo
grapes	unas uvas
grass	la hierba
gray	gris
great!	¡estupendo!
green	verde
guidebook	una guía
guitar	una guitarra
had, I	tuve
had, they	tuvieron
had, we	tuvimos

had, you	tuvo
hair	el pelo
hairdresser	la peluquería
half	medio
hall	el pasillo
ham	el jamón
hand	la mano
handkerchief	el pañuelo
happy	feliz
hard	duro
hat	el sombrero
have	tener
have, I	tengo
have, they	tienen
have, we	tenemos
have, you	tiene
he	él
he is	es, está
head	la cabeza
hear, I	oigo
hear, they	oyen
hear, to	oír
hear, we	oímos
hear, you	oye
heart	el corazón
heat, warmth	el calor
heel	el talón
hello	¡hola!
help, to	ayudar
here	aquí
herring	un arenque

high	**alto**
highway	la **autopista**
hill	la **colina**
hip	la **cadera**
horse	el **caballo**
hospital	un **hospital**
hot	**caliente**
hotel	un **hotel**
hour	la **hora**
house	la **casa**
how?	¿**cómo**?
how much?	¿**cuánto**?
hunger	la **hambre**
hurt, to	**doler**
husband	el **marido**
I	**yo**
I am	**estoy**
I am	**soy**
I ate	**comí**
I bought	**compré**
I bring	**traigo**
I came	**vine**
I can	**puedo**
I come	**vengo**
I could	**pude**
I eat	**como**
I feel	me **siento**
I fell	**caí**
I gave	**di**
I give	**doy**

I go	**voy**
I had	**tuve**
I have	**tengo**
I hear	**oigo**
I know	**sé; conozco**
I live	**vivo**
I'm sorry	**lo siento**
I made	**hice**
I make	**hago**
I prefer	**prefiero**
I put (past tense)	**puse**
I put (present tense)	**pongo**
I said	**dije**
I saw	**vi**
I say	**digo**
I see	**veo**
I spoke	**hablé**
I take	**tomo**
I think	**pienso**
I want	**quiero**
I wanted	**quise**
I was	**estuve**
I went	**fui**
ice cream	un **helado**
ice-cream parlor	la **heladería**
idea	la **idea**
if	**aunque**
ill	**enfermo**
in	**en**
in, inside (adverb)	**adentro**
include, to	**incluir**

inflamed	**inflamado**
injured	**lastimado**
insurance	el **seguro**
into	**adentro**
introduce, to	**presentar**
iron (clothes)	la **plancha**
island	la **isla**
Italy	**Italia**
jacket	una **chaqueta**
jam	la **mermelada**
January	**enero**
Japan	**Japón**
jaw	la **mandíbula**
jazz	el **jazz**
jeans	los **vaqueros** ?
jewelry	las **joyas**
job	un **empleo**
judge	el **juez**
juice	un **jugo**
July	**julio**
June	**junio**
keep, to	**retener**
key	la **llave**
kidney	el **riñón**
kilometer	el **kilómetro**
kitchen	la **cocina**
knee	la **rodilla**
knife	un **cuchillo**
know, I	**conozco; sé**

know, they	conocen; saben
know, we	conocemos; sabemos
know, you	conoce; sabe
laborer	el trabajador
lake	el lago
lamb	un cordero
lamp	una lámpara
larger	más grande
last	pasado
laundry	una lavandería
lawyer	el abogado
learn, to	aprender
leather	el cuero
leave, to	dejar
left	izquierda
leg	la pierna
lemon	el limón
lemonade	una limonada
less	menos
lessons	las lecciones
letter	la carta
lettuce	una lechuga
library	la biblioteca
license	la licencia
life	la vida
light bulb	la bombilla
lights (car)	los faros
line	la línea
linen	el lino
lion	el león

lips	los **labios**
list	la **lista**
listen, to	**escuchar**
live	**vivir**
live, I	**vivo**
live, they	**viven**
live, we	**vivimos**
live, you	**vive**
liver	un **hígado**
living room	una **sala**
lobster	una **langosta**
local	**local**
long	**largo**
look for, to	**buscar**
look, to	**mirar**
lose, to	**perder**
love, to	**amar**
low	**bajo**
luggage	el **equipaje**
lunch	la **comida**
lung	el **pulmón**
made, I	**hice**
made, they	**hicieron**
made, we	**hicimos**
made, you *He*	**hizo**
magazine	la **revista**
mail	el **correo**
mailbox	el **buzón**
make, I	**hago**
make, they	**hacen**

make, to	**hacer**
make, we	**hacemos**
make, you	**hace**
man	un **hombre**
manager	el **director**
many	**muchos**
map	un **plano**
March	**marzo**
market	el **mercado**
married	**casado**
match (game)	el **partido**
matches (fire)	las **cerillas**
materials	los **retales**
mathematics	las **matemáticas**
May	**mayo**
maybe	**quizás**
mayor	el **alcalde**
me	**mí**
mean, to	**significar**
measles	el **sarampión**
measurements	las **medidas**
meat	la **carne**
mechanic	el **mecánico**
medicine	la **medicina**
memory (faculty)	la **memoria**
memory	el **recuerdo**
merchant	el **comerciante**
message	el **mensaje**
meter	el **metro**
Mexico	**México**
midnight	la **medianoche**

mile	la **milla**
milk	la **leche**
milk shake	un **batido**
minister	un **ministro**
minute	el **minuto**
mirror	un **espejo**
moccasins	los **mocasines**
Monday	el **lunes**
money	el **dinero**
month	el **mes**
more	**más**
morning	la **mañana**
mother	la **madre**
motorcycle	la **motocicleta**
mountain	la **montaña**
mouse	el **ratón**
mouth	la **boca**
movie	un **cine**
muscle	el **músculo**
museum	un **museo**
mushrooms	los **champiñones**
music	la **música**
must	**deber**
mustard	la **mostaza**
my	**mi**
name (first)	el **nombre**
named, to be	**llamarse**
napkin	una **servilleta**
nation	la **nación**
near	**cerca**

neck	el **cuello**
necklace	un **collar**
need, to	**necesitar**
nephew	el **sobrino**
never	**nunca**
new	**nuevo**
newspaper	un **periódico**
next	**próximo**
night	una **noche**
nightgown	un **camisón**
no	**no**
noon	el **mediodía**
north	el **norte**
nose	la **nariz**
not	**no**
notions	la **mercería**
novel	la **novela**
November	**noviembre**
now	**ahora**
number	el **número**
nun	una **monja**
nurse	la **enfermera**
nursing	la **enfermería**
nylon	el **nilón**
occupations	las **ocupaciones**
ocean	el **océano**
October	**octubre**
of course	**claro**
of, from	**de**
official	el **oficial**

oil	el **aceite**
old	**viejo**
onion	la **cebolla**
only (adjective)	**solo**
only (adverb)	**solamente**
open	**abierto**
or	**o**
orange	**naranja**
orangeade	una **naranjada**
other	**otro**
out	**fuera**
owl	la **lechuza**
pain	el **dolor**
painful	**dolorido**
pair	un **par**
pan	la **cazuela**
panties	unas **bragas**
pants	los **pantalones**
paper tissues	los **tisús**
parakeet	el **perico**
park	un **parque**
park, to	**aparcar**
parrot	la **cotorra**
part	una **parte**
pastries	las **pastas**
peaches	los **melocotones**
pears	unas **peras**
peas	unos **guisantes**
pedestrian	el **peatón**
people	la **gente**

pepper	la **pimienta**
pharmacy	una **farmacia**
physics	la **física**
piano	un **piano**
pig	el **puerco**
pillow	la **almohada**
pills	las **píldoras**
pin	un **alfiler**
pineapple	la **piña**
pink	**rosa**
pistachio	el **mantecado**
place	el **lugar**
plate	un **plato**
platform	el **andén**
play	la **obra**
please	**por favor**
plums	unas **ciruelas**
pneumonia	la **pulmonía**
poached (cooking)	**escalfado**
police station	la **comisaría de policía**
poor	**pobre**
pork	un **cerdo**
porter	el **conserje**
post office	el **correo**
postcards	las **postales**
pot	el **pote**
potatoes	unas **patatas**
prefer, I	**prefiero**
prefer, they	**prefieren**
prefer, we	**preferimos**
prefer, you	**prefiere**

pregnant	**embarazada**
pretty	**lindo**
price	el **precio**
priest	un **sacerdote**
private	**privado**
problem	el **problema**
professions	las **profesiones**
program	un **programa**
psychology	la **psicología**
punch	un **ponche**
push	**empuje**
put, I (present tense)	**pongo**
put, I (past tense)	**puse**
put, to	**poner**
question	la **pregunta**
quiet	**tranquilo**
rabbi	un **rabí**
rabbit	un **conejo**
race	la **carrera**
radishes	los **rábanos**
rain	la **lluvia**
raincoat	un **impermeable**
raining	**lloviendo**
raw	**crudo**
rayon	el **rayón**
razor blades	unas **cuchillas**
read, to	**leer**
really	**realmente**
receipt	el **recibo**

red	rojo
refrigerator	la nevera
relatives	los parientes
rent, to	alquilar
repair, to	reparar
repeat that	repita eso
representative (gov't)	el representante
request, to	pedir
reserve, to	reservar
restaurant	un restaurante
rice	el arroz
rich	rico
right	derecha(o)
ring	un anillo
river	el río
roasted	asado
robin	el petirrojo
room	un cuarto; la habitación
rose	la rosa
rubbish	la basura
ruby	un rubí
rum	el ron
run, to	correr
Russia	Rusia
sad	triste
said, I	dije
sailboat	el velero
salad	una ensalada
salami	un salchichón
sale	la liquidación

salesman	el **vendedor**
salmon	el **salmón**
salt	la **sal**
same	**mismo**
sandals	las **sandalias**
sandwich	el **bocadillo**
Saturday	el **sábado**
sauce	la **salsa**
sausage	una **salchicha**
sautéed	**salteado**
saw, I	**vi**
say, I	**digo**
say, to	**decir**
scarf	la **bufanda**
school	la **escuela**
scotch	el **whisky escocés**
sea	el/la **mar**
seafood	los **mariscos**
seat	el **asiento**
second	**segundo**
see	**ver**
see, I	**veo**
self-service	el **autoservicio**
sell, to	**vender**
senator	el **senador**
send, to	**enviar**
September	**septiembre**
serve, to	**servir**
service	el **servicio**
several	**varios**
sharp	**agudo**

she	ella
she is	es, está
ship	el barco
shirt	la camisa
shoes	los zapatos
short	corto
shoulder	el hombro
show, to	mostrar
shower	la ducha
shrimp	unos camarones
signature	la firma
silk	la seda
silver	la plata
single (not married)	soltero
sink	el fregadero
sister	la hermana
sit, to	sentar
sitting	sentado
size (shoe)	el número
size (clothing)	la talla
skiing	el esquí
skin	el cutis
skirt	una falda
sleep, to	dormir
slice	un trozo, una rodaja
slip (clothing)	las enaguas
slippers	las zapatillas
slow	lento
slowly	despacio
small	pequeño
smaller	más pequeño

smoke, to	**fumar**
smoked	**ahumado**
snow	la **nieve**
soap	el **jabón**
soccer	el **balompié**
society	la **sociedad**
socks	los **calcetines**
soda	una **soda**
soft	**suave; blando**
sole (fish)	el **lenguado**
some	**alguno**
some (m.)	**unos**
some (f.)	**unas**
someone	**alguien**
something	**algo**
son	un **hijo**
song	la **canción**
soup	la **sopa**
south	el **sur**
Spain	**España**
Spanish	**español**
sparrow	el **gorrión**
speak, to	**hablar**
spice	la **especia**
spider	una **araña**
spinach	la **espinaca**
spoke, I	**hablé**
spoon	una **cuchara**
sports	los **deportes**
sprain	la **torcedura**
spring	la **primavera**

Húmedo
WET

squash (vegetable)	la **calabaza**
stairway	la **escalera**
stamp	el **sello**
start, to	**empezar**
stationery store	la **papelería**
steak	un **bistec**
steal, to	**robar**
steamed	**al vapor**
stew	un **estofado**
sting	una **picadura**
stockings	las **medias**
stomach	el **estómago**
stop	la **parada**
store	la **tienda**
storm	la **tormenta**
straight ahead/on	**todo derecho; todo recto**
strawberry	una **fresa**
stream	el **arroyo**
street	la **calle**
streetcar	el **tranvía**
strong	**fuerte**
student	el **estudiante**
subway	el **metro**
suede	el **ante**
sugar	el **azúcar**
suit	el **traje**
suitcase	la **maleta**
summer	el **verano**
Sunday	el **domingo**
sunglasses	las **gafas de sol**
sunny	**asoleado**

surname	el **apellido**
sweater	el **suéter**
sweet	**dulce**
swim	una **nadada**
swim, to	**nadar**
swimming pool	una **piscina**
symphony	la **sinfonía**
T-shirt	una **camiseta**
table	una **mesa**
take, I	**tomo**
take, they	**toman**
take, to	**tomar**
take, we	**tomamos**
take, you	**toma**
taxi	el **taxi**
tea	un **té**
teach, to	**enseñar**
teacher	el **maestro**
telegram	un **telegrama**
telephone	el **teléfono**
than	**que**
thank you	**gracias**
that	**esa**, **ese**
that's good	**está bien**
that's right	**exacto**
the (pl., m.)	**los**
the (s., m.)	**el**
the (s., f.)	**la**
the (pl., f.)	**las**
theater	el **teatro**

then	entonces
there	allí
there is	hay
they	ellas, ellos
they are	son; están
they ate	comieron
they bought	compraron
they bring	traen
they came	vinieron
they can	pueden
they come	vienen
they could	pudieron
they eat	comen
they go	van
they had	tuvieron
they have	tienen
they hear	oyen
they know	conocen; saben
they live	viven
they made	hicieron
they make	hacen
they prefer	prefieren
they take	toman
they think	piensan
they want	quieren
they wanted	quisieron
they went	fueron
they were	estuvieron
thing	una cosa
think, I	pienso
think, they	piensan

think, we	pensamos
think, you	piensa
third	tercero
thirst	la sed
this	esta, este
throat	la garganta
Thursday	el jueves
ticket	el billete
ties	las corbatas
tiger	el tigre
timetable	el horario
tires	los neumáticos
to	a
to answer	contestar
to arrive	llegar
to ask	preguntar
to be	estar; ser
to be able	poder
to be careful	tener cuidado
to be named	llamarse
to believe	creer
to bring	traer
to buy	comprar
to call	llamar
to cash	cobrar
to change	cambiar
to charm	encantar a
to come	venir
to continue	seguir
to dance	bailar
to depart	salir

to dream	soñar
to eat	comer
to enter	entrar
to estimate	estimar
to feel	sentir
to find	hallar
to follow	seguir
to get	obtener
to get up	levantarse
to give	dar
to go	ir
to have	tener
to hear	oír
to help	ayudar
to hurt	doler
to include	incluir
to introduce	presentar
to keep	retener
to learn	aprender
to leave	dejar
to like	gustar
to listen	escuchar
to live	vivir
to look	mirar
to look for	buscar
to lose	perder
to love	amar
to make	hacer
to mean	significar
to need	necesitar
to park	aparcar

to put	poner
to read	leer
to rent	alquilar
to repair	reparar
to request	pedir
to reserve	reservar
to run	correr
to say	decir
to see	ver
to sell	vender
to send	enviar
to serve	servir
to show	mostrar
to sit	sentar
to sleep	dormir
to smoke	fumar
to speak	hablar
to start	empezar
to steal	robar
to swim	nadar
to take	tomar
to teach	enseñar
to try	tratar
to understand	comprender
to use	usar
to wait	esperar
to walk	andar
to want	querer
to work	trabajar
to write	escribir
toasted	tostado

today	hoy
toilet	el servicio
toilet paper	el papel higiénico
toilets	los aseos
toll	el peaje
tomatoes	unos tomates
tomorrow	mañana
tongue	la lengua
too much	demasiado
tooth	el diente
toothpaste	la pasta de dientes
towel	una toalla
town	la ciudad
toys	los juguetes
traffic light	el semáforo
train	el tren
trip	el viaje
trout	una trucha
truck	el camión
true	verdadero
try, to	tratar
Tuesday	el martes
tulip	el tulipán
tuna	el atún
turbot	un rodaballo
ugly	feo
umbrella	un paraguas
uncle	el tío
underpants	los calzoncillos
understand, to	comprender

underwear	la **ropa interior**
United States	**Estados Unidos**
until	**hasta**
up	**arriba**
use, to	**usar**
vacation	la **vacación**
valley	el **valle**
vanilla	la **vainilla**
veal	la **ternera**
vegetable store	la **verdulería**
vegetables	las **legumbres**
very	**muy**
violin	un **violín**
vodka	una **vodka**
waist	la **cintura**
wait, to	**esperar**
waiter	el **camarero**
waiting	**esperando**
waitress	la **camarera**
walk	un **paseo**
walk, to	**andar**
wallet	la **cartera**
want	**querer**
want, I	**quiero**
want, they	**quieren**
want, we	**queremos**
want, you	**quiere**
wanted, I	**quise**
wanted, they	**quisieron**

wanted, we	quisimos
wanted, ~~you~~ He	quiso
was, I	estuve
washer	la **lavadora**
watch	un **reloj**
water	el **agua** (**f.**)
we	**nosotros**
we are	**estamos; somos**
we ate	**comimos**
we bought	**compramos**
we bring	**traemos**
we came	**vinimos**
we can	**podemos**
we come	**venimos**
we could	**pudimos**
we eat	**comemos**
we go	**vamos**
we had	**tuvimos**
we have	**tenemos**
we hear	**oímos**
we know	**conocemos; sabemos**
we live	**vivimos**
we made	**hicimos**
we make	**hacemos**
we prefer	**preferimos**
we take	**tomamos**
we think	**pensamos**
we want	**queremos**
we wanted	**quisimos**
we went	**fuimos**
we were	**estuvimos**

weak	**débil**
weather	el **tiempo**
Wednesday	el **miércoles**
week	la **semana**
well	**bien**
went, I	**fui**
went, they	**fueron**
went, we	**fuimos**
went, ~~you~~ *HE*	**fue**
were, they	**estuvieron; fueron**
were, we	**estuvimos; fuimos**
were, you	**estuvo; fue**
west	el **oeste**
wet	**húmedo**
what?	¿**qué**?; ¿**cuál**?
when?	¿**cuándo**?
where?	¿**dónde**?
where to?	¿**adónde**?
which?	¿**cuál**?
while	**mientras**
whiskey	un **whisky**
white	**blanco**
who?	¿**quién**?
who (whom)	**quien**
why?	¿**por qué**?
wife	la **esposa**
wind	el **viento**
window	la **ventana**
wine	un **vino**
winter	el **invierno**
with	**con**

with ice	con hielo
with me	conmigo
with you	contigo
without	sin
wool	la **lana**
word	la **palabra**
work, to	trabajar
world	el **mundo**
wound (injury)	la **herida**
wrist	la **muñeca**
write	escribir
write it down	escríbalo
yacht	el **yate**
year	el **año**
yellow	amarillo
yes	sí
yesterday	ayer
you	vosotros; ustedes
you (familiar)	tú
you (polite)	usted
you are (polite)	está; es
you are (familiar)	estás; eres
you ate	comió
you bought	compró
you bring	trae
you came	vino
you can	puede
you come	viene
you could	pudo
you eat	come

you go	va
~~you~~ had *H*	tuvo
you have	tiene
~~you~~ hear *H*	oye
you know	conoce; sabe
you live	vive
~~you~~ made *H*	hizo
~~you~~ make s *H*	hace
you prefer	prefiere
~~you~~ take s *He*	toma
you think	piensa
you want	quiere
you wanted	quiso
you went	fue
you were	estuvo
you're welcome	de nada
your (polite)	su
your (familiar)	tu
zoo	el zoológico

Spanish-English Glossary

a	to
abajo	down
abdomen	abdomen
abejas	bees
abierto	open
abogado	lawyer
abrelatas	can opener
abrigo	coat
abril	April
abuela	grandmother
abuelo	grandfather
aceite	oil
adelante	come in
adentro	in, inside (adverb)
adentro	into
¿adónde?	where to?
aeropuerto	airport
agosto	August
agua (m., con el)	water
agudo	sharp
águila (m., con el)	eagle
ahora	now
ahumado	smoked

ajo	garlic
al extranjero	abroad
al vapor	steamed
alcalde	mayor
alcoba	bedroom
Alemania	Germany
alérgico	allergic
alfiler	pin
alfombras	carpets
algo	something
algodón	cotton
alguien	someone
alguno	some
alicates	pliers
alimentación	food
allí	there
almacén	department store
almejas	clams
almohada	pillow
alquería	farmhouse
alquilar	to rent
alrededor de	around
alto	high
amar	to love
amarillo	yellow
ambiente	atmosphere
ambos	both
amigo	friend
ampolla	blister
andar	to walk
andén	platform

anillo	ring
animales	animals
ante	suede
antes	before
año	year
aparcar	to park
apartamento	apartment
apellido	surname
apio	celery
aprender	to learn
aquí	here
araña	spider
arenque	herring
aretes	earrings
arriba	up
arroyo	stream
arroz	rice
artículo	article
asado	roasted
asalto	assault
ascensor	elevator
aseos	toilets
asesinato	murder
asiento	seat
asoleado	sunny
aspirinas	aspirin
atún	tuna
aunque	if, although
autobús	bus
autopista	highway
autoservicio	self-service

avión	airplane
ayer	yesterday
ayudar	to help
azúcar	sugar
azul	blue
bacalao	cod
bahía	bay
bailar	to dance
bajo	low
balompié	soccer
banco	bank
baño	bathroom
barbacoa, a la	barbecued
barbero	barber
barco	ship, boat
barquillo	cone (ice cream)
basta	enough
basura	rubbish, garbage
bata	bathrobe
batería	battery
batido	milk shake
bebida	drink
biblioteca	library
bicicleta	bicycle
bien	well
billete	ticket
biología	biology
bistec	steak
blanco	white
blando	soft

blusa	blouse
boca	mouth
bocadillo	sandwich
bolso	bag
bomba	bomb
bombilla	light bulb
borbón	bourbon
botánico	botanical
botas	boots
bote	boat
botella	bottle
bragas	panties
brazo	arm
broche	brooch
bueno	good
buey	beef
bufanda	scarf
buscar	to look for
busto	bust
buzón	mailbox
caballo	horse
cabeza	head
cada	each
cadera	hip
café	coffee
café solo	black coffee
cafetería	café
caí	I fell
caja	check-out
calabaza	squash

calcetines	socks
calentura	fever
caliente	hot
calor	heat, warmth
calzoncillos	underpants
calle	street
cama	bed
cámara	camera
camarera	waitress
camarero	waiter
camarones	shrimp
cambiar	to change
caminar	to walk
camión	truck
camisa	shirt
camiseta	T-shirt
camisón	nightgown
Canadá	Canada
canario	canary
cáncer	cancer
canción	song
canela	cinnamon
cangrejo	crab
cara	face
cardenal	cardinal
carne	meat
carnicería	butcher
caro	expensive
carta	letter
cartera	wallet
carrera	race

casa	house
casado	married
caseta	cottage
catarro	cold (illness)
catorce	14
catre	cot
cazuela	pan
cebolla	onion
cena	dinner
cenicero	ashtray
cerca	near
cerdo	pork
cerezas	cherries
cerillas	matches
cero	0
cerrado	closed
cerveza	beer
cien	100
cigarrillo	cigarette
cinco	5
cincuenta	50
cine	movie
cintura	waist
cinturón	belt
ciruelas	plums
cita	appointment
ciudad	town, city
clarinete	clarinet
claro	of course
clásico	classical
clavel	carnation

clavos	nails (woodworking)
clérigo	clergyman
cobrar	to cash
coche	car
cocina	kitchen
codo	elbow
cola	glue
colegio	college, middle school
coliflor	cauliflower
colina	hill
collar	necklace
come	you eat
comedor	dining room
comemos	we eat
comen	they eat
comer	eat
comerciante	merchant
comí	I ate
comida	lunch; food
comieron	they ate
comimos	we ate
comió	you ate
comisaría de policía	police station
como	as (conjunction)
como	I eat
¿cómo?	how?
cómoda	dresser
compañía	company
compramos	we bought
comprar	to buy
compraron	they bought

compré	I bought
comprender	to understand
compró	you bought
con	with
con fiebre	feverish
con hielo	with ice
concejal	councilman
concierto	concert
condimentos	condiments
conejo	rabbit
congelados	frozen foods
conmigo	with me
conoce	you know
conocemos	we know
conocen	they know
conozco	I know
conserje	porter
contador	accountant
contestar	to answer
contigo	with you
continuo	continuous
coñac	brandy
corazón	heart
corbatas	neckties
cordero	lamb
correo	mail
correo	post office
correr	to run
corrida de toros	bullfight
corto	short
cosa	thing

cosméticos	cosmetics
coste	cost
cotorra	parrot
creer	to believe
cruce	crossroads
crudo	raw
¿cuál?	what?; which?
¿cuándo?	when?
¿cuánto?	how much?
cuarenta	40
cuarto	room
cuatro	4
cuchara	spoon
cuchillas	razor blades
cuchillo	knife
cuello	collar; neck
cuenco	bowl
cuenta	bill
cuero	leather
cuervo	crow
cuidado	care; careful!
cutis	skin
champaña	champagne
champiñones	mushrooms
chaqueta	jacket
cheque	check
chicle	chewing gum
China	China
chocolate	chocolate
chuletas	chops (meat)

dar	to give
de	of, from
de nada	you're welcome
deber	to have to, must
débil	weak
decir	to say
dedo	finger
dejar	to leave
demasiado	too much
dentadura	dentures
dentista	dentist
dependiente	clerk
deportes	sports
derecha(o)	right
desayuno	breakfast
desde	from
desodorante	deodorant
despacio	slowly
despejado	clear
después de	after
destornillador	screwdriver
desvío	detour
di	I gave
día	day
diamante	diamond
diarrea	diarrhea
diciembre	December
diecinueve	19
dieciocho	18
dieciséis	16

diecisiete	17
diente	tooth
dieta	diet
diez	10
diferente	different
digo	I say
dije	I said
dinero	money
Dios	God
dirección	address
director	manager
doble	double
doce	12
doctor	doctor
dólares	dollars
doler	to hurt
dolor	pain
dolorido	painful
domingo	Sunday
¿dónde?	where?
dormir	to sleep
dos	2
doscientos	200
doy	I give
dril	denim
droguería	drugstore
ducha	shower
dulce	sweet
durante	during
duro	hard

ejemplo	example
el	the (s., m.)
él	he
electricidad	electricity
elefante	elephant
ella	she
ellas	they (f.)
ellos	they (m.)
embarazada	pregnant
empaste	filling (tooth)
empezar	to start
empleo	job
empuje	push
en	at, in
enaguas	slip (clothing)
encantar(o)	to charm
enero	January
enfermería	nursing
enfermera	nurse
enfermo	ill
ensalada	salad
enseñar	to teach
entonces	then
entrada	entrance
entrar	to enter
enviar	to send
equipaje	luggage
equipo	equipment
es	he, she is; you are
esa	that

esas	those
escalera	stairway
escalfado	poached (cooking)
escoba	broom
escríbalo	write it down
escribir	to write
escuchar	to listen
escuela	school
ese	that
esmeralda	emerald
espalda	back
España	Spain
español	Spanish
espárrago	asparagus
especia	spice
espejo	mirror
esperando	waiting
esperar	to wait
espinaca	spinach
esposa	wife
esquí	skiing
esta	this
está	he/she is; you are
está bien	that's good
Estados Unidos	United States
estamos	we are
están	they are
estar	to be
estás	you are
este	east
este	this

estimar	to estimate
estofado	stew
estómago	stomach
estoy	I am
estreñimiento	constipation
estudiante	student
estupendo	great
estuve	I was
estuvieron	they were
estuvimos	we were
estuvo	you were
exacto	that's right
fácil	easy
falda	skirt
falso	false
familia	family
farmacia	pharmacy
faros	lights (car)
favorito	favorite
febrero	February
fecha	date
feliz	happy
feo	ugly
fiambres	cold cuts
finanzas	deposit
firma	signature
física	physics
flores	flowers
Francia	France
franela	flannel

fregadero	sink
frenos	brakes
fresa	strawberry
fresco	fresh
frío	cold
frito	fried
fruta	fruit
fue	you went
fuera	out
fueron	they went
fuerte	strong
fui	I went
fuimos	we went
fumar	smoke
gafas de sol	sunglasses
galletas	cookies
garganta	throat
gasolinera	gas station
gato	cat
gente	people
ginebra	gin
gobernador	governor
gobierno	government
gorrión	sparrow
gorro	cap
gracias	thank you
grande	big
grasa	fat
gripe	flu
gris	gray

guantes	gloves
guía	guidebook
guisantes	peas
guitarra	guitar
gustar	to like
habitación	room
hablar	to speak
hablé	I spoke
hace	you make
hacemos	we make
hacen	they make
hacer	to make
hago	I make
hallar	to find
hambre	hunger
hasta	until
hay	there is, there are
hecho	fact
heladería	ice-cream parlor
helado	ice cream
herida	wound (injury)
hermana	sister
hermano	brother
herramientas	tools
hervido	boiled
hice	I made
hicieron	they made
hicimos	we made
hierba	grass
hígado	liver

hija	daughter
hijo	son
hizo	you made
¡hola!	hello!
hombre	man
hombro	shoulder
hora	hour
horario	timetable
hormigas	ants
horneado	baked
hospital	hospital
hotel	hotel
hoy	today
hueso	bone
huevo	egg
húmedo	wet
hurto	theft
idea	idea
iglesia	church
impermeable	raincoat
incluir	to include
inflamado	inflamed
ingeniero	engineer
Inglaterra	England
inglés	English
invierno	winter
ir	to go
isla	island
Italia	Italy
izquierda	left

jabón	soap
jamón	ham
Japón	Japan
jardín	garden
jazz	jazz
joyas	jewelry
judías	beans (kidney)
jueves	Thursday
juez	judge
juguetes	toys
jugo	juice
julio	July
junio	June
kilómetro	kilometer
la	the (s., f.)
labios	lips
lago	lake
lámpara	lamp
lana	wool
langosta	lobster
largo	long
las	the (pl., f.)
lastimado	injured
lavadora	washer
lavandería	laundry
lecciones	lessons
leche	milk
lechuga	lettuce
lechuza	owl

leer	to read
legumbres	vegetables
lejos	far
lencería	dry goods
lengua	tongue
lenguado	sole (fish)
lento	slow
león	lion
levantarse	to get up
librería	bookstore
libro	book
licencia	license
limón	lemon
limonada	lemonade
limpio	clean
lindo	pretty
línea	line
lino	linen
liquidación	sale
lista	list
lo siento	I'm sorry
local	local
los	the (pl., m.)
lugar	place
lunes	Monday
llamada	call
llamar	to call
llamarse	to be named
llave	key
llegada	arrival
llegar	to arrive

lleno	full
lloviendo	raining
lluvia	rain
madre	mother
maestro	teacher
maíz	corn
maleta	suitcase
malo	bad
mañana	morning
mandíbula	jaw
mano	hand
manta	blanket
mantecado	pistachio
mantequería	delicatessen
mantequilla	butter
manzanas	apples
mar	sea
mareado	dizzy
margarita	daisy
marido	husband
mariposa	butterfly
mariscos	seafood
martes	Tuesday
martillo	hammer
marzo	March
más	more
más barato	cheaper
más grande	larger
más pequeño	smaller
matemáticas	mathematics

mayo	May
mayores	adults
me siento	I feel
mecánico	mechanic
media	half
medianoche	midnight
medias	stockings
medicina	medicine
medidas	measurements
mediodía	noon
México	Mexico
mejor	better
melocotones	peaches
memoria	memory (faculty)
menos	less
mensaje	message
mercado	market
mercería	notions
mermelada	jam
mes	month
mesa	table
metro	subway
metro	meter
mi	my
mí	me
mientras	while
miércoles	Wednesday
mil	1000
milla	mile
ministro	minister
minuto	minute

mirar	to look
mismo	same
mocasines	moccasins
monja	nun
montaña	mountain
moreno	brown
moscas	flies (insects)
mostaza	mustard
mostrar	to show
motocicleta	motorcycle
muchos	many
muebles	furniture
mundo	world
muñeca *Doll*	wrist
músculo	muscle
museo	museum
música	music
muy	very
nación	nation
nadada	swim (noun)
nadar	to swim
naranja	orange
naranjada	orangeade
nariz	nose
natillas	custard
necesitar	need
negocio	business
negro	black
neumáticos	tires
nevera	refrigerator

nieve	snow
nilón	nylon
niños	children
no	no, not
noche	night
nombre	first name
norte	north
nosotros	we
novecientos	900
novela	novel (book)
noventa	90
noviembre	November
novio	boyfriend
nublado	cloudy
nueve	9
nuevo	new
número	number; size (shoe)
nunca	never
o	or
obra	play
obtener	to get
océano	ocean
ochenta	80
ocho	8
octubre	October
ocupaciones	occupations
oeste	west
oficial	official
oído	ear (hearing)
oigo	I hear

oímos	we hear
oír	to hear
ojo	eye
once	11
oreja	ear
oro	gold
oso	bear
otoño	autumn
otra vez	again
otro	other
oye	you hear
oyen	they hear
padre	father
pájaros	birds
palabra	word
palo	club
paloma	dove
pan	bread
pana	corduroy
panadería	bakery
pantalones	pants
pañería	drapery
pañuelo	handkerchief
papel higiénico	toilet paper
papelería	stationery store
par	pair
para	for
parada	stop
paraguas	umbrella
parientes	relatives

parque	park
parrilla, a la	broiled
parte	part
partido	match (sports)
pasado	last
paseo	drive; walk
pasillo	hall
pasta de dientes	toothpaste
pastas	pastries
patatas	potatoes
peaje	toll
peatón	pedestrian
pecho	chest
pedir	to request
película	film
peligro	danger
pelo	hair
peluquería	barbershop, hairdresser
pensamos	we think
pepino	cucumber
pequeño	small
peras	pears
perder	to lose
perdone	excuse me
perico	parakeet
periódico	newspaper
pero	but
perro	dog
pesca	fishing
pescadería	fish market
pescado	fish

petirrojo	robin
piano	piano
picadura	sting
pie	foot
piensa	you think
piensan	they think
pienso	I think
pierna	leg
píldoras	pills
pimienta	pepper
piña	pineapple
piscina	swimming pool
piso	floor
pistola	gun
plancha	iron (clothes)
plano	map
planta	floor
plata	silver
plátanos	bananas
plato	plate
playa	beach
pobre	poor
pocos	few
podemos	we can
poder	to be able
pollo	chicken
polvoriento	dusty
pomelo	grapefruit
ponche	punch
poner	to put
pongo	I put (present tense)

por	by
por favor	please
¿por qué?	why?
porque	because
postales	postcards
postre	dessert
pote	pot
precaución	caution
precio	price
preferimos	we prefer
prefiere	you prefer
prefieren	they prefer
prefiero	I prefer
preguntas	questions
preguntar	to ask
presentar	to introduce
primavera	spring
primero	first
primo	cousin
privado	private
problema	problem
profesiones	professions
programa	program
próximo	next
psicología	psychology
pude	I could
pudieron	they could
pudimos	we could
pudo	you could
puede	you can
pueden	they can

puedo	I can
puerco	pig
puerta	door
pulmón	lung
pulmonía	pneumonia
pulsera	bracelet
puse	I put (past tense)
que	than
¿qué?	what?
quemadura	burn
queremos	we want
querer	to want
queso	cheese
quien	who (whom)
¿quién?	who?
quiere	you want
quieren	they want
quiero	I want
química	chemistry
quince	15
quise	I wanted
quisieron	they wanted
quisimos	we wanted
quiso	you wanted
quizás	maybe
rábanos	radishes
rabí	rabbi
rápido	fast
rapto	kidnapping

ratón	mouse
rayón	rayon
realmente	really
recibo	receipt
reclamaciones	complaints
recuerdo	memory
regalo	gift
regla	ruler
reloj	watch
remolachas	beets
reparar	to repair
repita eso	repeat that
repollo	cabbage
representante (gov't)	representative
reservar	to reserve
respuesta	answer
restaurante	restaurant
retales	materials
retener	to keep
revista	magazine
rico	rich
rifle	rifle
riñón	kidney
río	river
robar	to steal
robo	robbery
rodaballo	turbot (fish)
rodajas	slices
rodilla	knee
rojo	red

ron	rum
ropa interior	underwear
ropero	closet
rosa	pink; rose
rubí	ruby
Rusia	Russia
sábado	Saturday
sabe	you know
sabemos	we know
saben	they know
sacerdote	priest
sal	salt
sala	living room
salchicha	sausage
salchichón	salami
salida	exit, departure
salir	to depart
salmón	salmon
salsa	sauce
salteado	sautéed
sandalias	sandals
sangre	blood
sarampión	measles
sartén	frying pan
sé	I know
sección	department
seco	dry
sed	thirst
seda	silk

seguir	to follow, continue
segundo	second
seguro	insurance
seis	6
sello	stamp
semáforo	traffic light
semana	week
senador	senator
sentado	sitting
sentar	to sit
sentir	to feel
septiembre	September
ser	be
servicio	toilet; service
servilleta	napkin
servir	to serve
sesenta	60
setenta	70
sí	yes
sidra	cider
siempre	always
sierra	saw
siete	7
siglo	century
significar	to mean
silla	chair
sin	without
sinfonía	symphony
sobres	envelopes
sobrino	nephew

sociedad	society
soda	soda
sofá	couch
solamente	only
sólo	only
soltero	single (not married)
sombrero	hat
somos	we are
son	they are
soñar	to dream
sopa	soup
sordo	dull
sostenes	bras
sótano	basement
soy	I am
su	your
suave	soft
sucio	dirty
sueño	dream
suéter	sweater
sujetador	bra
sur	south
taladro	drill
talla	size (clothing)
talón	heel
también	also
tambor	drum
tapas	appetizers
tarde	afternoon

taxi	taxi
té	tea
teatro	theatre
teléfono	telephone
telegrama	telegram
tenedor	fork
tenemos	we have
tener	have, to
tener cuidado	to be careful
tengo	I have
tercero	third
ternera	veal
tía	aunt
tiempo	weather; time
tienda	store
tiene	you have
tienen	they have
tigre	tiger
tintorería	dry cleaner
tío	uncle
tisús	paper tissues
toalla	towel
tobillo	ankle
tocino	bacon
todo	everything
todo recto	straight on (ahead)
toma	you take
tomamos	we take
toman	they take
tomar	to take

tomates	tomatoes
tomo	I take
torcedura	sprain
tormenta	storm
tornillos	screws
torta	cake
tos	cough
tostado	toasted
trabajador	laborer
trabajar	to work
trae	you bring
traemos	we bring
traen	they bring
traer	to bring
traigo	I bring
traje	suit
tranquilo	quiet
tranvía	streetcar
tratar	to try
trece	13
treinta	30
tren	train
tres	3
triste	sad
trozo	slice
trucha	trout
tú	you (familiar)
tu	your (familiar)
tulipán	tulip
tuve	I had

tuvieron	they had
tuvimos	we had
tuvo	you had
un	a (masculine)
una	a (feminine)
uña	fingernail
unas	some (f.)
uno	1
unos	some
usar	to use
usted	you (polite)
ustedes	you (plural)
uvas	grapes
va	you go
vaca	cow
vacación	vacation
vainilla	vanilla
vajilla	crockery
valle	valley
vamos	we go
van	they go
vaqueros	jeans
varios	several
vaso	glass
veinte	20
velero	sailboat
venda	bandage
vendedor	salesman
vender	to sell

vengo	I come
venimos	we come
venir	to come
ventana	window
veo	I see
ver	see
verano	summer
verdadero	true
verde	green
verdulería	vegetable store
vestido	dress
vi	I saw
viaje	trip
vida	life
viejo	old
viene	you come
vienen	they come
viento	wind
viernes	Friday
vine	I came
vinieron	they came
vinimos	we came
vino	you came
vino	wine
violín	violin
vive	you live
viven	they live
vivimos	we live
vivir	live
vivo	I live
vodka	vodka

vosotros	you (plural)
voy	I go
whisky	whiskey
whisky escocés	scotch
y	and
yate	yacht
yo	I
zanahorias	carrots
zapatillas	slippers
zapatos	shoes
zoológico	zoo

The Science Behind the Subliminal Method

THE FOLLOWING EXPLANATION gives the scientific basis of this program's method; however, this information is not essential for using this program.

The subliminal method is based on the "bilingual-dichotic" method (Aarons et al., 1990, 1992, 1998, 1999). In this method, the foreign word is channeled to your right ear and the English word to your left ear at about the same time. Next, the foreign word goes to both of your ears; you consciously pay attention to the foreign word while reading both the English and the foreign words from a list.

Repetition of the foreign word provides two different opportunities for you to learn. Presenting both the English and the foreign word simultaneously in the first opportunity maximizes your semantic association of the two through automatic conditioning, à la Pavlov. The second opportunity focuses on helping you learn the pronunciation of the foreign word while yielding a faster learning of the word pair. The two intervals—first within the same word pair and then between them and the next word pair—provide occasions for you to say the foreign word aloud.

On a practical level, this method will help you learn because you will need less time to master the basic lexicon; your mind will wander less while you study; and you will improve your recall of the foreign words, thereby reducing the "tip of the tongue" phenomenon and the need to hunt for the meaning of words in a pocket dictionary or an electronic translator.

Studies have shown that your lack of awareness of materials presented when you are asleep also occurs in certain conditions while you are awake. In both cases, the information is presented above your threshold for hearing in the awake state, but you don't perceive it consciously. This lack of awareness can include a subliminal reception that occurs in certain conditions of dichotic listening. In this type of listening, two different sound patterns are simultaneously presented separately to your right and left ears.

Your right and left ears are more strongly connected to the opposite cerebral hemispheres than to their own hemispheres. Each side of your brain is activated for different specialized language processing—analytic on the left and gestalt on the right. Moreover, monaural and dichotic verbal stimulation reveal an inherent perceptual asymmetry favoring words coming from your right side (Geffen and Quinn 1984). The strong right-ear advantage for speech processing can help you perceive and temporarily store sounds in an unfamiliar foreign word. It is recognized, however, that the plasticity of your nervous system allows you to control some of your auditory perception by shifting your attention between your ears. Nevertheless, your conscious attention is absorbed in a foreign word entering by way of your right ear. This leaves unused neural capacities to provide for subliminal or unconscious reception of verbal input in your left ear. The significant right-ear advantage in dichotic listening associated with left-ear input is basic to this program's method.

Your performance is enhanced by ergonomic design, which aligns structure with function. For example, round doorknobs are easily used to open a door because they fit the human hand—the contour at the interface is optimized. Likewise, matching the presentations of words with your anatomical and psychological structures and processes facilitates your learning. Your initial perception of foreign words when you first begin learning requires discrete phonemic analysis. In contrast, you tend to perceive words in your native language as gestalts or holistically. Selective attention is required for the former; you can perceive the latter automatically without paying attention to it.

References

Aarons, L. 1990. The bilingual-dichotic method for learning a foreign-language vocabulary. *Applied Cognitive Psychology* 4:383–92.

Aarons, L. Bilingual-dichotic learning of foreign-language vocabulary: visual cued recall and phrases. In *Proceedings of the 22nd International Congress of Applied Psychology, Vol. 3: Social, Educational, and Clinical Psychology*, edited by Motoaki, H., J. Misumi, and B. Wilpert (Kyoto, Japan; Hillsdale, NJ: Lawrence Erlbaum Associates, 1992), 182.

Aarons, L. 1998. Wordlists and the bilingual-dichotic method. *Agoralanguage Newsletter* 4, no. 3 (May 1998).

Aarons, L., A. Aarons, and J. H. Lachman. 1999. Mental effort in learning with the bilingual-dichotic method. *Agoralanguage Newsletter* 5, no. 2 (February 1999).

Geffen, G., and K. Quinn. 1984. Hemispheric specialization and ear advantages in processing speech. *Psychological Bulletin* 96:273–91.